W9-AWW-905

EMPOWERMENT OF A RACE

EMPOWERMENT OF A RACE

The Revitalization of Black Institutions

JESSE J. LEWIS
AND JOHN HAYMAN

Black Belt Press
MONTGOMERY

The Black Belt Press
P.O. Box 551
Montgomery, AL 36101

Library of Congress Cataloging-in-Publication Data

Design by Randall Williams
Printed in the United States of America
        5 4 3 2 1

*The Black Belt, defined by its dark, rich soil, stretches across central Alabama. It
was the heart of the cotton belt. It was and is a place of great beauty, of extreme
wealth and grinding poverty, of pain and joy. Here we take our stand, listening to
the past, looking to the future.*

This book is dedicated to

JESSE J. LEWIS, JR.

a man of great promise and accomplishment who was tragically killed in an automobile accident in 1995. He would have been proud of this book, and moreover, he would be proud of the fact that his father is giving all of the royalties he earns from this book in equal parts to the National Urban League, the NAACP, the Southern Christian Leadership Conference, and the United Negro College Fund.

CONTENTS

FOREWORD

JOSEPH E. LOWERY

A BOOK about empowering a *race* is an ambitious project. Nothing in the world of technology, including walking on the moon, is more complex, multi-faceted, mysterious, elusive, and precipitous as analyzing and understanding "the race problem," let alone offering a solution. The authors, however, courageous fellows that they are, have taken on such a task and the book will provide interesting and provocative reading, especially for those whose interest in the subject is beyond the ordinary. A principal premise of the book seems to be that following the success of the civil rights movement in abolishing segregation based on race, and winning the right to vote, black leaders abandoned the masses on an isle of helplessness while the ships (called institutions) of desegregation sailed into the mist and were later torpedoed by missiles labeled integration. The authors deposit most of the blame for the plight of the masses on the shoulders of black leaders, who convinced them that the government owed them something but they were not sure what it was nor where it could be found. While many readers will take issue with the pontifications of the sideline quarterbacks, they will, nevertheless, find the book interesting and even challenging.

This commentator has preached for years that *authentic integration is not the systematic movement of all things black to all things white, but the emphatic movement of all things wrong to all things right.* So, I have little problem joining the lament for the loss and weakening of black institutions, including black-owned businesses. In education, we have witnessed the loss of black principals and teachers who provided caring environments for learning and growth. We still face the threat of losing historically black colleges. We need to strengthen most of these institutions, for the truth is that 40 percent of African Americans who graduate from college come from these institutions in spite of the fact that they enroll only 25 percent of black students.

The authors seem unduly influenced by Negroes who absolve the *system* of any responsibility for poverty that affects blacks and millions of whites in this nation. Most people who were on welfare prior to the unproven welfare-to-work experiment were white. The entire nation has suffered from policies that export jobs while expanding poverty. The *system* is not designed to achieve full employment with livable wages. The *system* still produces a society where less than 15 percent of the people control more than 80 percent of the wealth. The apologists who totally absolve the system are engaged in oppressive politics and parasitical economics.

To define affirmative action as preferences and quotas is deceptive and diabolical. Authentic affirmative action is being intentional about remedying what was intentionally afflicted. To abandon intentionality in closing the gap is to abandon the national commitment to justice and equity. If two fingers on your hand are infected, common sense dictates that you give those fingers intentional ministration lest you imperil the well-being of the whole darn hand!

Having hammered the gauntlet, let me say that there can be no gainsaying of the fact that the "battle is in our hands." The coalition of conscience—civil rights, religion, students, workers, minorities, women— must intensify efforts to finish the unfinished task of "redeeming the soul of America." In 1985, we initiated a movement called "liberation lifestyles" that challenged us not to fall victim to the assault from without by our fault from within. If we are to be "free at last," we must embrace lifestyles that are free from self-hate, free from dependency on alien substances, free to teach our dollars some sense, free to turn TO each other and not ON each other, free to strengthen our families, free to be activists in achieving radical change!

I believe the authors are saying a similar thing in their own way. But don't take my word for it, read the book for yourself. You'll enjoy it. I did!

Dr. Joseph E. Lowery is Chairman of the Black Leadership Forum, Founder-President Emeritus of the Southern Christian Leadership Conference, Chairman of the Georgia Coalition for A Peoples Agenda, and a nationally syndicated columnist.

PREFACE

T HIS is a moment of hope in the long struggle for equality. As we approach a new century, the United States has the greatest opportunity in history to solve its most intransigent problem, the problem of achieving full citizenship for black citizens. At the same time there is danger that the opportunity will be missed, and the third of black Americans who reside in the inner city will sink further into despair and hopelessness. This book is a call to the recommitment and action needed to assure that black America finally is fully empowered.

Africans first came to the New World about the same time as Europeans. The Spanish brought black slaves in 1509, only seventeen years after Columbus. Twenty black people landed at the English settlement at Jamestown in 1619, twelve years after the colony's founding. They did not come to Jamestown as slaves but as indentured servants, and after they fulfilled the terms of their indenture, they were free, with the full rights of Englishmen. Africans helped to build the United States, along with Anglo-Saxons, Hispanics, Orientals, and many others. All of these, by their labor, are the true owners of this land. It is one of the tragedies of history that our founding fathers did not immediately apply the great principles of freedom and equality to all of the country's inhabitants. Playing politics, they let the curse of slavery remain, and a heavy price is still being paid two centuries later.

When the Voting Rights Act was signed in 1965, about 5 percent of African Americans were in the middle class. Today the proportion is 40 percent. An increase from 5 percent to 40 percent by a major population group in such a brief period is unique in history. The number of black elected officials in the United States has increased in the same period from a tiny handful to more than 8,000. For these and other reasons, African Americans are in a much stronger position than at any time in the past to control their own destiny. They have reached what we believe are critical masses of political and economic power. An essential is to use the power at hand to revitalize a number of black institutions.

These matters are discussed in detail in *Empowerment of a Race*. The co-authors are a biracial team. One of us, Jesse Lewis, is black, and the other, John Hayman, is white. Together we enumerate and support our arguments for optimism, discuss the things that still need to be done, and attempt through our example to demonstrate the trust, respect, and cooperation needed between racial groups in the United States.

Our purpose in writing the book is twofold. First, we will take the most honest measure we can of the state of black America at this time in American history. Second, we will outline in some detail the steps we believe are necessary for black Americans to revitalize institutions and reach a higher level of empowerment. Most of these steps are fundamentally the responsibility of black citizens. They cannot be accomplished, however, unless the larger society plays an essential facilitating role, and we will comment briefly on this point.

Central objectives of the immediate future for black Americans must include strengthening of the black church and other institutions; self-sufficiency, responsibility, morality, and unity; improved education; effective participation in the political system; increased entrepreneurship and economic advancement; and further movement into a broadened mainstream. Steps which must be taken by the majority population and by government may be generalized under the broad category of assuring finally a full measure of social, legal, and economic justice.

As President Clinton and many others remind us, we stand at a threshold as the world enters a new century and a new millennium.

Vernon Jordan recently noted that there are two paths we can take as we move forward. The first is the path of integration, progress toward building multiracial societies, and more harmonious interracial discourse. The second is continued polarization, with black-white friction and growing racial disadvantage.

Surely we all know that our society must take the first path. We have come too far and worked too hard to allow ourselves to be stopped because we cannot give up that last bit of distrust or anger or hostility. The fight will continue to be hard, but for the first time there is reason to believe that victory is within reach. This is no time to rest on past accomplishments. It is a time to keep fighting, to stay united, and to avoid the temptation to focus on self and neglect the larger responsibilities of community.

What we propose ultimately is reconciliation, mutual respect in diversity, true equality in the broad sense implied in the Declaration of Independence and the Bill of Rights, and at the highest level, unity. We use "diversity" in the sense of accommodating multiple races, cultures, political outlooks, and religions within our boundaries and political system.

Our original plan was to revise Jesse Lewis's 1985 book, *Survival of a Race*. As we moved into the project, we realized so much has changed in the last decade that a complete rewrite was necessary. To eliminate any confusion with the original book, and to express our beliefs about the current state of affairs more accurately, we decided to change the name to *Empowerment of a Race: The Revitalization of Black Institutions*. The original book was the inspiration for this one and motivated our work together.

We are indebted to several people for their support. First are our wives, Helen Lewis and Clara Ruth Hayman, who put up with neglect and the brunt of irritation during intense writing, and who still inspired us and urged us on. Special thanks are due to Dr. Dan Landis, University of Mississippi, and Dr. Marvin Dawson, retired from Mercer University, who critiqued the manuscript and made valuable suggestions for improvement. Shawn Castle of Jesse J. Lewis and Associates did the cover illustration, and Ted Tucker Photography handled portraits. Cheryl English, chief secretary at *The Birmingham Times,* was helpful in facilitating communication and in assisting with reference material.

Randall Williams and the staff at Black Belt Press supported this project from its early stages, and they did their usual fine job in reviewing the text and suggesting needed revisions. As publication time drew near and we shared a mutual desire to have the book out in time for Black History Month in 1999, they went beyond the call of duty in getting it done.

JESSE J. LEWIS
JOHN HAYMAN

Empowerment of a Race

PROLOGUE

Institutions and
the State of Black America

AS a new century and a new millennium approach, African Americans stand at a transitional moment. For the first time in American history, full empowerment is within their reach, but a number of black institutions must be revitalized for empowerment to occur. There is strong evidence that many of the difficulties black Americans experienced after the Voting Rights Act was passed in 1965 resulted from the absence of effective supporting institutions. This has been a special problem for inner-city blacks, who comprise about one-third of the national African American population. It is a problem which contributed to the deterioration of their circumstances during in the 1970s, 1980s, and early 1990s.

We use "institution" in the broad sense. An institution is a group of people who work and act together for some common purpose, people who are bound by enduring relationships and whose common behaviors are important in some aspect of social, political, economic, or religious life. Thus a family coming together each year for a reunion can be seen as an institution, as can the United States Supreme Court, the National Urban League, and the Notre Dame football team. In everyday life, institutions function as support mechanisms which provide stable relationships, help generate a sense of self, define the world and one's place in it, and allow people to feel safe, secure, and valued.

Prior to the Civil Rights Movement, black Americans developed their own institutions because they had to, and these covered all aspects of their social life. They developed their own clubs and associations, their own churches, their own businesses. They had the Negro League in baseball, their own theater, and their own music. As the legal battles were won and segregation fell, these institutions tended to crumble and weaken.

Just why is not altogether certain, though one factor seems to have been the naive assumption that blacks would move into institutions previously restricted to whites and no longer needed their own. Black institutions were ignored. A portion of the African American community moved successfully into the middle class, but another portion was left behind, with even less support than before.

What happened is aptly described by Linda Pearce, who left Wilmington, North Carolina, after college to work for the Library of Congress but who returned to North Carolina in 1980. Speaking of her school in Wilmington and her life experiences, she said, "We were in a cocoon bathed in a warm fluid, where we were expected to excel. And then something called desegregation punctured it. We went from our own land to being tourists in someone else's."[1]

Pearce's analogy is apt. The treatment of black citizens by American society before the Civil Rights Movement was terribly wrong, and fundamental changes were needed. But social change moves slowly and haphazardly, particularly if its substance is intertwined with culture. When you are a tourist in another land, you need help for the adjustments you have to make, and you need assistance from the natives in easing you into their way of life. In short, you need supporting institutions to make possible your transition. Some of the most critical institutions are church, family, education, involvement in decisions about government, and the process of making a living, either as an employee or business owner. In addition, you still need contact with the way of life you left even if you have lived in a new country for decades.

THE FAILURE to provide needed institutions for black citizens is not a new problem in American history. It happened on a large scale twice before, to the country's great detriment. When the Constitution was written in 1787, the United States tragically missed a great opportunity to make blacks full citizens. Bowing to political expediency, the framers allowed slavery to continue, even though the great majority of them knew it was wrong. They knew that slavery violated the words and spirit of the Declaration of Independence and the Constitution. They left for another generation the task they should have completed, and one result seventy years later was the Civil War, which ripped the country to pieces and almost destroyed it.

The second failure occurred after the Civil War. Passions to do good were still strong in the years just after the war's end. Reconstruction legislation was passed, Freedmen's Bureaus were set up, schools were started, and other steps were begun to help the former slaves achieve full citizenship. In a short time, however, the country lost interest, and the efforts which had been started amounted to very little. The freed slaves were each promised forty acres and a mule, but this promise was kept for only a few. The newly freed blacks, who were without education or experience in managing life independently, were cast adrift to fend for themselves.

In 1876, barely ten years after the war's end, Reconstruction officially ended, and it was almost a total failure. People intent on maintaining white supremacy were in full control of the governments of all the former Confederate states. Efforts to legally deprive African Americans of many of the basic rights of citizenship proceeded, and by the beginning of the 20th century, all of the Southern states had "segregation" constitutions which accomplished this result. Many of the provisions were tested and approved by the U.S. Supreme Court. Treating citizens in this way was evil, no matter how you look at it, but it did have the effect of forcing blacks to develop their own social institutions and their own subculture.

A half century later the modern Civil Rights Movement began, and over a ten-year period, it succeeded in ending all legal barriers to equality and full citizenship. It also had the effect of weakening or destroying many black institutions and removing support mechanisms needed for self-esteem and feelings of security and stability, particularly among the urban poor.

Many black Americas were cast adrift, just as their ancestors had been 100 years before. The strong rhetoric of civil rights leaders told people that they had been deprived of things that were rightly theirs, and it also stated that the larger society owed them something. These statements were true in many respects, but they did not clarify what it was the larger society owed — nor where one's own responsibility began and ended.

The rhetoric helped to create among some blacks a debilitating condition referred to by certain writers as "victim mentality." Victim mentality is a feeling of being the helpless victim, out of control of one's destiny. It is debilitating because it prevents people from recognizing actual cause and effect relationships in their lives. Because they see themselves as helpless, with no control, they blame every circumstance in which they find themselves on outside forces, and they fail to understand their own contribution to their situation. They fail to take responsibility because of their inability to see that they can effect change for themselves.

One of the reasons that victim mentality flourishes among lower class blacks is the lack of supporting institutions. It is the product of alienation, of being adrift in a world which appears to offer no hope.

People in this situation are deprived of opportunities in a very real sense. This is especially devastating to young people, particularly those who are poor. They do not get a good education because of inadequate facilities, because they do not internalize the importance of learning, and because there is no one to help and encourage them when they have problems in school. Poor education and the scarcity of black-owned businesses assure they do not have adequate employment opportunities or positive role models. Their moral development is stunted because the church does not reach out to them and family ties are weak.

MATERIAL IN this book will confirm that the problem of inadequate institutions, presented in these few pages in broad sweep, does in fact exist. Solving this problem is a necessary prerequisite to the empowerment of black America in national life. The institutional revitalization of which we speak is largely a matter internal to and the responsibility of the black community. A respected black leader, quoted later in the text, states the plain fact that blacks must take responsibility for their own destiny if there is to be positive change in their condition.

This will occur within the larger meaning of diversity and pluralism which has evolved in American society. Black Americans, like others who came to these shores, should be aware of, take pride in, and be guided by their cultural heritage. This means a black consciousness in politics, in economics and education, and in other important institutions. Coupled with pluralism is understanding that the future of us all is irrevocably bound with the future of America.

The revitalization of black institutions will not in itself assure that empowerment occurs, because the larger society plays an essential, facilitating role. It must avoid the pitfalls of racism and reaction, and it must provide a nurturing environment. America must do what it has failed to do many times in the past and assure that black citizens enjoy the same rights as other citizens: maximum freedom consistent with the maintenance of order, equal treatment before the law, and full opportunity to develop according to individual abilities, energy, and motivation. We also believe it essential that our country, guided by the fundamental conviction that all humans are equal in the sight of God, must continue its efforts to make full opportunity a reality by assisting those who are born into disadvantaged circumstances.

This is the right moment in American history to take the steps which are advocated. It is a time of hope as a new century approaches. Black Americans as a whole have made astounding progress during the last thirty-five years, but a substantial black underclass persists. The last hurdle in gaining full and equal participation in the society remains. The full empowerment of black America is a step whose time has come, and the revitalization of black institutions is essential to that step.

Black America at Century's End: A Transitional Moment

If there is no struggle, there is no progress to favor freedom. Those who profess to favor freedom and yet deprecate agitation are men who want crops without plowing up the ground. They want rain without thunder and lightning; they want the ocean without the awful roar of its many waters. This struggle may be a moral one; or it may be a physical one; or it may be both moral and physical; but it must be a struggle. Power concedes nothing without a demand.

FREDERICK DOUGLASS

What, then, is the dark world thinking? It is thinking that as wild and awful as this shameful war was, it is nothing to compare with that fight for freedom which black and brown and yellow men must and will make unless their oppressions and humiliation and insult at the hands of the White World cease. The Dark World is going to submit to its present treatment just as long as it must and not one moment longer.

W. E. B. DU BOIS

AS THE 21st century approaches, the United States of America stands at a moment of hope and of opportunity finally to solve its most difficult problem. The country has been plagued since its founding by an inability to deliver to black Americans the freedom and opportunity which is its basic promise to all citizens. Now, in the late 1990s, there is reason to believe that a critical mass in the move toward equality is being achieved. But part of the fight remains. As always, grasping freedom and holding it requires organized, vigilant, intelligent effort.

In the Civil Rights Movement, black Americans freed themselves from American apartheid, a legalized system of caste and color separation.[1] Jim Crow was dead. When President Lyndon Johnson signed the Voting Rights Bill on August 6, 1965, it seemed in that moment of triumph that full citizenship was at hand. The optimism lasted less than a week. On August 11, terrible riots broke out in the Watts section of Los Angeles, and they were among the most destructive racial violence in American history.

The Watts riots came as a profound shock to many. Could it be that smashing Jim Crow in the South was not enough? As it turned out, Watts was only a beginning, a sign that the complex, deep-seated, persistent problem of race relations in American society would last many more decades. Watts signaled that it was no longer a Southern problem, but a problem of the whole nation. The Civil Rights Movement had eliminated legal denial of rights, but it had not made blacks equal in economic standing nor in other aspects of life. In fact, the changed environment required major adjustments in social interaction and new efforts at self-identification. It led in some instances to social disorganization.

More than thirty years have passed since the end of the great civil rights battles of the 1950s and 1960s, and blacks have made remarkable progress in a number of areas. Included are substantial movement into the middle class, participation in the political system, and involvement in entertainment, education, athletics, and other aspects of American life. Progress during this period has been unprecedented historically in scope and speed. Yet a substantial proportion of the black population has not shared in the movement forward.

If Martin Luther King Jr. could come back to America today, he would find his famous dream is unrealized for roughly a third of black Americans. He would find:

1. A nation in which there was a turn to the right in political sentiment and attempts to pull back from commitment to civil rights and equal opportunity in education and employment.
2. A nation where 20 million people do not have enough food.
3. A nation where teenage black unemployment is higher than 50 percent, twice as high as for other teenagers.

4. A nation where black-on-black crime is running rampant.

5. A nation in which one third of all black people under 30 are involved in some way in the criminal justice system.

What happened? One of the clearest explanations of a significant part of the problem was given by Rose Sanders, a Harvard-educated black lawyer from Selma, Alabama:

> When the Civil Rights Movement ended, institutional building didn't begin. If the Civil Rights Movement had expanded to the point of building institutions or of improving institutions to take care of the needs of the people, then I don't think you would have the violence and despair we have today. Instead, people were so elated to have the victory, to have thePresident of this country say, "We shall overcome," that many people thought the battle was over. That's where we made our critical mistake.[2]

BLACK PEOPLE won the civil rights battle in the sixties. They lost the equal opportunity wars in the seventies, eighties, and nineties by neglecting to build and improve institutions. At century's end, prosperity and a changing political climate have brought full empowerment within reach, but a necessary step to achieving it, the revitalization of fundamental black institutions, remains.

I. Background

To understand what has happened, it is instructive to examine briefly the history of race relations in the United States. The attempt to achieve equality had a long history before King assumed leadership of the modern Civil Rights Movement in Montgomery, Alabama, in 1955. It began, in fact, with efforts to end slavery at the founding of the republic. This effort reached its climax with the Civil War and the dramatic changes it wrought.

Then, as in 1965, advocates of full equality believed they were close to reaching their goal. The constitutional and legal changes of the time were possible because the conscience of the nation was caught up in the mighty struggle. Sooner than anyone expected, however, the country lost interest. Reconstruction, the attempt to remake the South according to democratic principles of equality before the law, economic justice, and full participation in the political process effectively ended by 1870.

During the remaining years of the 19th century, leaders in the South proceeded to undo most of what had been achieved and to restore white supremacy in all walks of life. By 1905, all of the former Confederate states had "Jim Crow" constitutions — documents which legally deprived blacks of most of the basic rights of citizenship. The rest of the nation, believing blacks inferior, was content to look the other way and allow the heart of progress made through the Civil War to be squandered.

In this we see an almost haunting parallel to what has happened since the Civil Rights Movement ended. Intense activity catches the nation's attention, and gross injustices activate the collective conscience, leading to a great leap forward in constitutional and legislative change. Almost as fast, the nation lapses into a state of comfort in which righteous causes are forgotten, and people choose to live with as little challenge and as little annoyance as possible.

The moral is clear enough: Social change is never easy and will not occur without being constantly pushed. W.E.B. Du Bois, a great civil rights leader in the early years of this century, noted that social change requires "blunt complaint, ceaseless agitation, unfailing exposure of dishonesty and wrong. This is the ancient, unerring way to liberty," Du Bois said, "and we must follow it."[3] Du Bois predicted then that the struggle of the 20th century would be the struggle of the color line. Sadly, his prediction proved to be true.

It is a lasting disgrace and a blight on the history of the United States of America that we have allowed the matter of black inequality to continue uncorrected to the present day. President Clinton stated recently that if we solve the problems associated with diversity, the future for this country is unlimited. One might add that if we don't solve these problems, we may find ourselves relegated to the trash heap of history because we couldn't live up to our ideals.

In this book, we will examine in more detail the current state of race relations in the United States, recent historic events which produced our current situation, and institutions in society which have an important role to play in reaching empowerment. Based on this examination, we will outline the steps toward institutional revitalization we believe can help carry the country forward.

II. Progress Under Six Presidents

More important civil rights legislation was passed under Lyndon Johnson than under any other President. But Johnson's thrust in this direction became weakened and confused because of his conduct of the Vietnam war and the strong reaction to it. The Democrats, who had carried the banner of civil rights since the days of Harry Truman, split into factions and engaged in destructive internal warfare. Their great civil rights champion Hubert Humphrey was compromised because, as Vice President, he was forced to defend Johnson's war policies. The ultimate result was Humphrey's loss to Republican Richard M. Nixon in the 1968 Presidential election.

Nixon gained fame in his early years as a hatchet man for the Republicans, a person who readily violated the civil rights of early political opponents, such as Jerry Voorhis and Helen Douglas. As Vice President, he did the dirty work, playing the heavy to Eisenhower's Mr. Clean. By the time Nixon became President, he had a reputation as a brilliant but complex character of questionable moral fibre.

Nixon went into the 1968 election with a politically motivated Southern strategy which aimed to gain Southern votes by playing to their conservative religious and racial views. Among other promises, he pledged to install strict constructionist judges in the federal courts, judges who would not be activist in promoting citizen's rights. A key part of the Southern strategy was the old cry that things were moving too fast. After he took office in 1969, Nixon remarked at a press conference that those who wanted "instant integration" were as "extremist" as those who wanted "segregation forever."[4]

Under pressure from Senator Strom Thurmond and other Southern political leaders, the Nixon administration began early in 1969 to pull back on the Department of Health, Education and Welfare (HEW) guidelines on school integration and to talk of extensions for Southern school districts seeking more time to desegregate. The pace of government intervention to guarantee equal treatment for all citizens slackened. Whether the general rate of progress was acceptable is a matter of debate. Blacks certainly did not think it was. Aside from that, a trend started which proved to be much more insidious in the long run. This was the deliberate move by Nixon and the Republicans to make the judiciary more conservative.

Since the *Brown v. Board of Education* decision in 1954, the event which triggered the Civil Rights Movement, the federal courts had been very proactive in the civil rights struggle. Southerners and other reactionaries complained loud and long throughout the next fifteen years that the courts were going beyond their constitutional authority.

Shortly after he took office in 1969, Nixon had a vacancy to fill on the Supreme Court. He considered Alabamian Frank Johnson, a Republican and a federal district judge, but Southerners blocked serious consideration of Johnson because of his progressive record on civil rights issues. Later that year, Nixon bowed to Southern pressure and nominated G. Harrold Carswell, a forty-nine-year-old district judge in Florida, to fill the vacancy.

On more than a dozen occasions, Carswell had been reversed unanimously by the Fifth Circuit in civil rights cases. After Nixon submitted his name for the Supreme Court, the National Leadership Conference for Civil Rights sent a memorandum to the Senate Judiciary Committee protesting that the nominee "has been more hostile to civil rights cases than any other federal judge in Florida." A reporter dug up the fact that, as a candidate for the legislature in Georgia in 1948, Carswell had said, "I yield to no man . . . in the firm, vigorous belief in the principles of white supremacy, and I shall always be so governed." The debate over the

Carswell nomination was bitter, and in the end he was rejected by the Senate.[5]

A day later, Nixon, with Attorney General John Mitchell at his side, said in a press conference, "I have reluctantly concluded that — with the Senate as it is presently constituted — I cannot successfully nominate to the Supreme Court any federal appellate judge from the South who believes as I do in the strict construction of the Constitution."

In the six years he was President, Nixon succeeded through his appointments to make the federal courts more conservative, a trend which would resurface in the Reagan Administration. As a result, the federal courts began to strike down certain affirmative action plans on the principle that blacks cannot be given job preference over whites because of past discrimination.

On the positive side, school desegregation proceeded and effectively encompassed the whole South. Pockets of resistance remained, it is true, and the private segregationist school movement accelerated. But there was no longer any question that desegregation was the law of the land. Black voting rights were protected and expanded. Black citizens cast their ballots in unprecedented numbers and became a potent political force. The number of black officeholders increased dramatically.

Nixon endorsed the concept of affirmative action, in the sense of taking positive steps to try to bring the number of minority employees in government-related organizations to levels similar to their proportions in the population. The Nixon administration introduced the concept of numerical hiring goals and timetables, imposed the requirement that individual employers prepare written affirmative-action plans, and introduced minority-hiring quotas for federal construction contractors.

Richard Nixon resigned as President on August 9, 1974, under intense pressure caused by the Watergate scandal — the first President in the country's history to leave office in this manner.

VICE-PRESIDENT Gerald Ford assumed the Presidency in September 1974. Almost immediately, he asked the Secretary of Labor to accelerate the obligation of funds under the Comprehensive Employment and

Training Act, and he seemed to take a more progressive stance on civil rights matters. During the Ford Administration, a statutory prohibition against sex discrimination in federally aided schools and colleges was translated into the Title IX regulations. The Office of Education announced the "Lau Remedies," which required school districts with twenty or more children who spoke a language other than English to teach them in their primary language and to provide them with bicultural education.

Some progress was made, but to blacks these actions seemed half-hearted. The Urban League expressed dissatisfaction with Ford's performance, and it also observed that the people did not seem to care. "Of all the disappointments experienced by Black America the past year," it concluded, "none was more disheartening than the widespread indifference of the American people to the plight of minorities and the poor."[6]

The same report found that, despite increased voting and election successes, blacks felt that they exercised little decision-making power in the larger political scene and did not participate effectively in the political process. An Urban League survey found employment to be the primary concern among blacks. The second greatest concern was inner-city revitalization and safe, sanitary housing for the poor and people with moderate incomes. Quality, career-oriented education was third.

On the positive side, there was a significant increase during the Ford administration in the number of black professionals, increased voting sophistication among blacks, improved media coverage, attitude changes among young blacks and whites, and some gains in housing integration.

WHEN President Jimmy Carter took office in January 1977, the rhetoric of the last two Administrations seemed to have convinced much of the American public that discrimination was a thing of the past. An article in *Integrated Education* observed that, "The federal machinery that Congress established in the 1960s to eradicate denials of civil rights remained largely intact, but it had grown rusty from disuse."[7] With Carter came some optimism that the new President might bring "the same type of moral leadership that led the nation to accept the legitimacy of black demands for equality during the sixties."

Carter made clear that he would seek to bring more women and minorities onto the federal bench. In his first year, he appointed blacks to fill two of ten appeals court vacancies and named a woman to one of the twenty-one openings on the district court bench. The President's Memorandum of July 1977 on enforcement of Title VI of the Civil Rights Act of 1964 was the strongest support for this critical compliance tool since the law was signed by President Johnson.

Key changes took place under Carter in the government's definition of and actions in support of affirmative action. The Administration promoted, and the Supreme Court gave its blessing to, race-consciousness, contract set-asides, and quotas as affirmative action tools. In the important *Bakke* case, the Justice Department defended the constitutionality and necessity of race-conscious measures to undo the effects of past discrimination, and the Supreme Court concurred. Previously, the official position was to be "color blind."[8]

The Justice Department changed the definition of "discrimination" to a statistical imbalance as contrasted to its previous insistence that discrimination has to result from willful action. Discrimination was implied, in other words, by the fact that the makeup of the work force in an organization was not in proportion to the makeup of the population.

In another move, focus was placed on groups as contrasted with individuals, and as a result, government actions affecting the economic well-being, status, and power of identifiable groups came to be viewed and debated as civil rights issues.

The Civil Rights Division of the Justice Department became very aggressive in pushing the new affirmative action agenda. The burden of proof fell on employers to prove that they were not discriminating. A downside was that organizations had to file large numbers of forms to establish their compliance with new regulations.

Well before the 1980 election, there was ample evidence of popular and Congressional dissatisfaction with the new aggressive stance of the Justice Department. The new definition of affirmative action was highly controversial and became an issue in the 1980 election.

At the same time, the American people expressed mounting displeasure with group favoritism. A Gallup survey found that only 11 percent of all respondents (including just 12 percent of women and 30 percent of nonwhites) condoned "preferential treatment in getting jobs and placed in college," while 82 percent of all men, 80 percent of women, and 55 percent of nonwhites believed that "ability, as determined by test scores, should be the main consideration."[9]

On the positive side, Carter was clearly a friend of the Civil Rights Movement and did his best to help the movement forward. Equalizing strategies were fully elaborated for the federal government. Many federal agencies were able to rebuild, reorganize, and establish new standards defining equal opportunity in areas where such standards were long overdue.

HEW issued regulations to carry out the law protecting handicapped persons from discrimination and new guidelines for equal opportunity in colleges and universities. The agency helped alleviate delays in handling civil rights investigations, and there was an agreement to collect from public school systems data needed to detect violations.

Very important was the Carter effort to reverse the Nixon and Ford efforts to make the courts more conservative and less proactive. Aided by the 1978 Omnibus Judgeship Act that gave him 152 new federal judgeships, Carter ended his four years in office having appointed forty women, thirty-eight blacks, and sixteen Hispanics to the federal bench. In a great performance, Carter had made more appointments from these groups than any other President.

As the 1980 election approached, Carter's strong civil rights stand created an issue which was clearly elaborated in the platforms of the two major parties. The Democratic platform stated, "Our commitment to civil rights embraces not only a commitment to legal equality, but a commitment to economic justice as well."

The Republican platform took a clear shot at quotas and at the definition of discrimination as statistical imbalance with these words: "Equal opportunity should not be jeopardized by bureaucratic regulations and decisions which rely on quotas, ratios, and numerical requirements to exclude some individuals in favor of others, thereby rendering such regulations and decisions inherently discriminatory."

THE ELECTION of 1980 resembled that of 1920 in that the people wanted a return to "normalcy." In 1920, voters had tired of Woodrow Wilson's preaching, of their intense emotional involvement in a great cause, of sacrifice. In 1980, they had recently gone through the Civil Rights Revolution, the Vietnam War, Watergate, and Jimmy Carter's calls to born-again fervor in pursuing righteousness. So they elected their movie-star idol, and in the words of Julian Bond, they embarked on a festive party, the greatest beneficiaries of which, it turned out after eight years, were America's rich.[10]

After Reagan's election, a report of the conservative Heritage Foundation, "Mandate for Leadership," became an unofficial statement of the new administration's agenda. It stated in principle that "color-blindness" should again become the standard for employers, admissions, and federal agencies, and that "discrimination" should be defined as willful action and not statistical imbalance.

The Department of Justice, led by Attorney General Edwin Meese and William Bradford Reynolds, director of the Civil Rights Division, repudiated the civil rights enforcement policies of the six previous Democratic and Republican administrations. Laws prohibiting discrimination in voting, education, employment, housing, and the Federal funding of programs were all targets. Congress, controlled by the Democrats, successfully blocked most of the attempts to weaken such laws. Significantly, Reagan was the first President since Andrew Johnson in 1866 to veto a civil rights bill, the 1988 Civil Rights Restoration Act. Congress overrode his veto.

In a move which created an impassioned backlash, the Reagan administration decided to grant tax exemptions to segregated church schools. While this appealed to the religious right, it clearly challenged the constitutional guarantee of the separation of church and state. An observer called it "purely and simply a matter of old-fashioned racism." The most notorious case involved segregated Bob Jones University. The administration's efforts to get tax exemption for the university were rejected by the Supreme Court.

Statistics from the last years of the Reagan Presidency show that:

- The percentage of young families who owned their own homes fell for the first time since the Depression.
- For Americans whose skins were black or brown, the poverty rate went up while median family income went down.
- There was a sharp increase in the proportion of black children living in poverty, in single-parent households, and in homes where the family head was unemployed.
- The drug problem increased. There was a crack cocaine invasion of inner-city neighborhoods, and AIDS emerged as a special health concern.
- The number of poor households increased by more than 25 percent, while the number of low-rent housing units declined by 20 percent. One third of poor blacks lived in substandard housing, about two-and-a-half times the proportion of poor whites living in such circumstances.
- Monies spent for entitlement programs such as welfare and food stamps were reduced at the same time that the number of Americans under the poverty level increased by one million.

Ronald Reagan was in office eight years, and circumstances gave him an unusual opportunity to make judicial appointments. By happenstance, a large number of Supreme Court justices and lower court judges reached retirement age during Reagan's two terms. Taking advantage, Reagan rekindled the effort of Nixon and Ford to make the federal judiciary more conservative, and he succeeded far more than his Republican predecessors.

At the end of his term, President Reagan had appointed three Supreme Court justices, and he elevated one of them, William Rehnquist, to Chief Justice. In a familiar 5-4 pattern, Reagan's three Supreme Court appointees joined two other conservative justices to make it harder to file anti-discrimination suits, to win anti-bias suits, and to sustain challenged affirmative-action agreements.

Benjamin Hooks, then NAACP executive director, commented that, "Night has fallen on the Court as far as civil rights are concerned." Ralph G. Ness, Executive Director of the Leadership Conference on Civil Rights, said, "I believe the new five-person majority on the Supreme Court poses the gravest threat to civil rights and civil liberties in America today."[11]

Reagan appointed 41 percent of the judges on the federal appeals courts and 39 percent of those on federal district courts. He appointed a majority of the judges on circuit courts. The greatly altered judicial system dictated in significant measure what the agenda of the Civil Rights Movement would be for the immediate future.

Ralph Ness speculated that few Americans fully comprehended how the biggest success of the rightwingers in the Reagan administration — the capture of the Federal judiciary — could adversely affect the law of the land well into the 21st century.

The record makes clear that President Reagan and his associates in the Executive branch of the federal government were not friends of the Civil Rights Movement. Despite their views and their sometime negative approach, however, many positive things were accomplished in American society in the 1980s to bring the country closer to racial equality.

Time and again, huge bipartisan majorities in Congress reaffirmed the nation's basic civil rights laws and remedies and rejected the extremism of the Reagan Administration. The Democratic 100th Congress, which served in 1987 and 1988, compiled one of the most successful and productive civil rights records in the nation's history.

Blacks were elected to high offices all over the United States, including such Southern cities as Atlanta, Birmingham, and Memphis, and their right to serve was accepted by the great majority of the populace even in the Deep South.

The electoral victories of Douglas Wilder as governor of Virginia and David Dinkins as mayor of New York City were also steps in the long process of removing America's racial barriers in elections. These victories proved that a significant number of white citizens based their votes on the competence and ideas of the candidates and were willing to vote for African Americans.

To summarize the Reagan legacy, this President had the greatest effect on civil rights of any who served in the office after Lyndon Johnson. It wasn't all bad. If blacks happened to be in the upper middle class or higher, their prospects improved along with the rest of the well-off. But if they were poor — and a much larger proportion of blacks were poor than whites — their prospects declined. Generally, Reagan's influence was strongest in three key areas. First, at the end of his term, the poor people of the country were worse off than they had been in 1980; second, the federal judiciary was turned profoundly in a conservative direction; and third, and perhaps most insidious, a disdainful attitude toward people who were different became respectable. Rosalyn Carter captured the latter point poignantly when she observed that the Reagan Administration "makes us feel comfortable with our prejudices."

THE YEAR 1989 began as a time of hope for African Americans, because it brought with it the Presidency of George Bush, who pledged greater openness and a fair-minded approach to civil rights. At an early news conference, Bush asserted that he was "strongly committed to civil rights and equal opportunity," and he maintained that the Justice Department assured him that recent Supreme Court rulings did not question affirmative action or minority outreach efforts.

The new President announced a strong program to combat drugs, and on September 5, 1989, he announced in a televised speech that his administration planned to combat the drug problem with an additional $2.2 billion in fiscal 1990. Congress fought over the amount but in large measure supported the administration's anti-drug efforts.

On other civil rights issues, it soon became clear that the President's views differed from the majority in Congress. On June 13, 1989, he vetoed an increase in the minimum wage. The House overrode his veto, but the override failed in the Senate. Later in 1989, the administration tried, under the guise of cutting the deficit, to restrict increases in federal assistance in child care. As it turned out, Bush battled extensively with the Democratic Congress. This resulted on one hand in his failure to get even half of his own legislative measures passed. On the other hand, he effectively managed to stifle the civil rights efforts of Congress. After two years in office, Bush became the first Republican President since Eisenhower to make it through a Democratic Congress without an override. He had used twenty-one vetoes. The effects of the conservative turn in the courts continued to be felt. Early in Bush's term, the more conservative Supreme Court ruled that enforcing quotas in affirmative action was unconstitutional.

Probably the most significant civil rights actions during the Bush administration dealt with the issues of affirmative action and the definition of "discrimination." The executive branch of government continued its conservative reaction to positions which had been taken by the Carter administration. The big word in this fight was "quotas."

By a single vote, the Senate in October 1990 failed to override Bush's veto of a sweeping civil rights bill. It was the first defeat of a major civil rights bill in the last quarter century. The bill would have made it easier to prove job discrimination. Bush and business groups contended that the bill would cause companies to adopt hiring quotas for women and minorities and would be subject to frivolous lawsuits.

Bush vetoed a revised bill in 1991, and again he withstood an override attempt. The bill was intended to offer workers more protection against bias, largely by reversing a series of Supreme Court decisions that narrowed the reach of anti-bias laws. Republicans had been pounding away with the message that the measure would force employers to use quotas to avoid costly lawsuits. They struck a nerve with white constituents worried about holding onto their jobs in a frail economy.

In the election year of 1992, Bush got into a fight with Congress over school choice. Bush and Education Secretary Lamar Alexander supported the use of federal funds for private schools. They argued that children should be able to "vote with their feet," leaving bad schools for better schools. This, they said, would spur schools to improve through competition for children. Congress prevailed in the debate by refusing to support even a single demonstration program involving private school choice.

The country fared well enough economically under Bush until the spring of 1992, when it went into recession. The Brady Bill, the first national gun-control bill in history, was passed in June of 1991 after some acrimonious debate. Bush supported the bill, as did Senate Minority Leader Robert Dole.

In summary, while Bush's record in civil rights was better than his predecessors, his administration continued the assault on affirmative action, it supported the federal courts in their conservative thrust, and it generally paid homage to his party's right wing in such matters as aid to private schools and aid for the poor. Overall, actions of the Bush and Reagan administrations constitute what we call the "Reagan/Bush White Counter-Revolution."

BILL CLINTON, governor of Arkansas, defeated Bush in 1992 and took the Presidency the following January. Clinton had taken liberal positions on social issues throughout his political career, and he expanded black power in the United States with his personnel choices as President. Several key appointments were to cabinet-level posts. These included Ronald H. Brown as Secretary of Commerce, Hazel R. O'Leary as Secretary of Energy, Mike Espy as Secretary of Agriculture, Jesse Brown as Secretary of Veteran Affairs, and Joycelyn Elders as Surgeon General. Clifton Wharton, Jr., was named Deputy Secretary of State. More recent appointments include Alexis Herman as Secretary of Labor and Dr. David Satcher as Surgeon General.

These actions placed African Americans among the elite policymakers in the United States.

Clinton has had the burden of an unfriendly Congress. The Democrats had a majority during his first two years, but their margin was so thin that Southern conservatives, joining Republicans, could prevent any legislation they didn't like. The midterm elections of 1994 placed solid Republican majorities in both the House and the Senate. The Republican "Contract with America" fizzled for the most part, but it took the initiative from the President in proposing bold new actions in areas the rightwingers would not support.

President Clinton is well into his second term. He is under strong assault from the far right, and he has established himself squarely in the middle of the political spectrum. His stance irritates those both on the far right and the far left, though he continues to have high approval ratings for his performance as President.

Early in 1998, Clinton came under investigation for alleged sexual misconduct with a former White House intern, and he was attacked viciously by Special Prosecutor Kenneth Starr. A few months later, he admitted both the sexual encounter and deliberately lying about it to the American people. In this regrettable display of poor judgment, he played into the hands of his enemies. As this book goes to press, the House of Representatives is beginning an impeachment inquiry, and if it votes to impeach, a trial will be held in the Senate. At this writing, his future as President was in the hands of Congress as the constitutional process for dealing with undesirable conduct by elected officials was being played out.

Bill Clinton's legacy could very well be his effort to help America progress in its civil rights struggle. This will depend on which of the proposed changes are put in place and how his remaining days in office are played out. If it were not for the sexual allegations against Clinton and his unfortunate decision to lie publicly, he might go down as one of the great Presidents. No one can say that Clinton has not faced up to the problems of this country. He has made an outstanding contribution to Medicaid and Medicare, saved the Social Security system, created a budget surplus for the first time in thirty years, and maintained a prosperous economy, and he has fought hard for the rights of gays and lesbians.

III. Major Issues Today

As the country moves into the last two years of the 20th century, its most perplexing problem — achieving full equality for black Americans

— remains unsolved. Great progress has been made the last thirty years in that large numbers of blacks have entered the mainstream, but at the same time, devastating things have happened to the less fortunate, to those still mired in poverty. An underclass has developed, marked by family breakdown and large increases in youth violence.

At this stage, the issues which must be addressed fall into three major categories. The first consists of such traditional areas of concern as employment, education, and family integrity. The second involves a redefinition of the national government's role in light of recent history. Third is the necessity to revitalize the fight to win equality.

A national debate on the provision of health service has raged the last four years, with conservatives trying to move toward more privatization and liberals cautioning that this would leave the poor unprotected. Standing out in stark clarity is the fact that the average life expectancy for black males is 65, eight years less than for white males. The poor simply do not receive the same level of health care as others in this society, and the question remains unanswered as to whether health care in the United States is to be considered a fundamental right as it is in some other industrialized nations.

Perhaps the most basic of the traditional concerns is employment. The black unemployment rate is two-and-a-half times the white rate, and the gap is growing. Half of all black kids grow up poor. And poor kids have high dropout rates that make them either unemployable or trainable only for entry-level jobs and at enormous expense.

Before World War II, just five percent of blacks were in the middle class. Today the figure is closer to 40 percent, an enormous increase. But the restructuring of the economic system has resulted in the disappearance of the well-paid manufacturing jobs that pulled blue-collar workers, black and white alike, into prosperity. Good jobs now require skills that schools in poor neighborhoods generally do a dismal job of teaching.

The breakdown in the black family and the rise of the drug culture, a terribly self-destructive trend, has developed largely in the last thirty years. Richard Lycayo points out one of the consequences. For young black men, he notes, the major cause of death is murder. Nearly one in every three black men between twenty and twenty-nine years of age is behind bars, on probation, or on parole.[12]

Family breakdown feeds poverty, which feeds more family breakdown. Devoted fathers are needed in homes to interrupt this diabolical cycle. But, as Harvard Professor Cornel West notes, fathers must be able to support their families. "Even the most devoted dads can't get jobs where there are none or start a business where there's no start-up capital."[13] The breakdown of the family and the rise in inner-city crime thus interact strongly with employment and education issues.

Many of the greatest problems are based in poverty. Julian Bond calls this, "The last item on the civil rights agenda — economic justice." The right to decent work at decent pay is as basic to freedom as the right to vote, Bond says. This right still has not been adequately addressed.

There has been a wide call for black entrepreneurship and for individual initiative among blacks. But these qualities can only pay off when society provides a level playing field. Equality in this sense is an essential by-product of economic justice. The rightwing view is that aggressive, affirmative government efforts to end discrimination are unnecessary because individual blacks hold within themselves the key to their own advancement.

A MAJOR question today is what society, acting through its government, should do to achieve economic justice. Since 1965, the federal government, largely under the initiative of the Democrats, has used affirmative action and the welfare state as major strategic thrusts in the effort to achieve racial equality. During the same period, the black underclass developed. A fundamental question is the extent to which the strategic thrusts of the government contributed to the new problems.

There seems little doubt that welfare somehow took a wrong turn. A strong case can be made that much of the demoralization of minorities can be traced to sixty years of federal policy that has made people more dependent on government. Both Republicans and Democrats agree that welfare and other aid programs need to be transformed so that they lift people up instead of creating a new type of degrading dependency.

Affirmative action is the area of civil rights enforcement that has stirred the greatest controversy and incurred the deepest resentment. All Presidents since Nixon said they supported affirmative action, but the major question is what they meant operationally.

Is it possible for affirmative action to be excessive and counterproductive? Is it fair, for example, to call an action "discriminatory" when it cannot be shown that the actor intended to discriminate? Can an action with unequal effects on different racial groups be reasonably termed "discriminatory" without reference to motivation or intent?

Just as basic is the question of whether rights accrue to groups as well as to individuals. The great mandate throughout the Civil Rights Movement was for equal individual opportunity within a colorblind society. As government action expanded, however, color awareness was recognized officially. Republicans have supported the elimination of legal barriers to full equality. They have balked, however, at government efforts to better the condition of designated groups.

The debate remains. Is the federal government responsible for taking positive steps to redress past wrongs to identifiable groups, or is it to take a *laissez-faire* attitude, confine itself basically to assuring individual rights, and otherwise let the chips fall where they may? As Julian Bond has observed, if the *laissez-faire* view prevails, those who have had a head start in the economic race obviously enjoy a great advantage.[14]

IT IS essential at this time to revitalize the effort to achieve full equality in the United States. Americans seem exhausted by the effort expended to come this far, and embittered by the new brand of race-based obsessions that have developed along the way. The nation is eager to embrace the benefits of yesterday's civil rights achievements, while it rejects or ignores the obligation to take the final steps and make full equality a reality.

Lani Guinier says that aggressive advocacy is essential to insure that black interests are taken seriously. This is the same point made by W. E. B. Du Bois almost a century ago. Technical, formal access to the political process is not enough to guarantee even good-faith representation.

Blacks must participate fully in the political process, and black voters must demand post-election accountability of all of their representatives, black as well as white.

Participating fully in the political process is an essential point, but it is at the same time a dilemma. Nationally, blacks constitute some 13 percent of the population, and they still tend to live in enclaves, with slow dispersion into mixed areas. Neighborhood integration is the ideal way to achieve integration in institutions such as schools. The result, however, is diluted black voting strength. Gerrymandering to prevent blacks from having representation, as in the Tuskegee case in the late 1950s, was wrong. By the same token, logic tells us that gerrymandering to guarantee black representation may also be questionable.

Several congressional districts which were set up to guarantee black victories have come under legal attack in recent years and have been eliminated by the Supreme Court. Further, there is a debate about the ultimate effectiveness of such gerrymandering. Including blacks in a single district dilutes progressive strength in other districts.

Alabama is a case in point. The state has one liberal black congressman and seven far-right white congressmen. Without the awkward gerrymandering which produced this result, there could very well be four or five moderate whites, and the black congressman could very well win anyway. This point was brought home in the 1998 elections when black voters helped defeat incumbent governor Fob James.

Black people in America are trying to find a leader. They haven't had a broadly recognized leader since Martin Luther King, and they don't know what actions to take. This was confirmed in a poll taken at the Million Man March. Interviewees said they felt there was a shortage of leaders, and eight in ten said the march would make Louis Farrakhan more influential among blacks.[15]

We believe blacks would like to go with Farrakhan, but they're afraid he is too controversial. They would like to go with Colin Powell, but they don't know him and therefore don't trust him.

During the Reagan years, blacks began to vote at levels approximating their numerical strength in the community. As their voting numbers increased they began to see the ballot as an important tool for pursuing the civil rights agenda. On the other hand, many blacks feel stifled by the traditional two-party approach. It seems to them that, no matter how they vote, whites still govern and tend to put issues of interest to blacks on the back burner.

In the 1988 Presidential race, Jesse Jackson's second place finish had great symbolism, but it did not secure blacks a place at the bargaining table. To keep the faith, blacks expect political fairness. This means a fair opportunity to choose their representatives, a fair shake in administrative enforcement that protects minority voting rights, and a fair share of substantive, legislative policy outcomes.

The last few years have seen an unfortunate polarization of racial attitudes in the United States. Many whites think blacks have won their rights and need to clean up their own act, while many blacks are unable to overcome their sense of outrage and suspicion.[16] A *Washington Post* survey taken at the Million Man March found a strong undercurrent of racial tension.

Our politics have moved toward racial polarization. Blacks have seen themselves cast, sometimes openly, as the welfare freeloader or the affirmative-action hire. The South, once the stronghold of the Democratic Party, has followed the Dixiecrats into the Republican ranks, largely because of racial issues. "Liberal," a term that once meant fairness, equality, and racial justice, has developed into the hated "L" word.

Contributing to racial polarization is a widespread feeling of economic insecurity. As the shift to a global, information-based economy accelerates, people sense that they do not have the job security of the past. They don't really understand the cause, and they look for scapegoats. This gives rise to new levels of prejudice toward anyone who is different and is perceived as competition in the work place.

IV. The Challenge of the Million-Man March

The Million Man March was held in the nation's capital on October 16, 1995. It was described by organizers as "a day of atonement and unity for black men nationwide." Those present pledged themselves to take greater responsibility for themselves and their families. There was a strong call for spiritual renewal. While Louis Farrakhan's leadership made the march controversial, observers generally called it an outstanding success.

A news release by an organization of black psychologists stated that the March signified the further reawakening of the sense of unity, purpose, efficacy, and self-worth of black men, who have been the target of historical forces designed to "denigrate black manhood and dehumanize all black people."

It was, the psychologists said, "a 'Black Holy Day' which said to ourselves, our children, and the world that our very existence is worthy of affirmation."

The psychologists' report continued, "We challenge the participants and African-American men everywhere to choose self-respect over personal degradation; truth, honesty, and hard work over crime and violence; definitions of manhood where support and protection of family and respect for women are valued over irresponsible sexual gratification; commitment to excellence in the acquisition of knowledge over dropping out or halfhearted efforts in school; life and negotiation over killing and gang violence; voter registration over voter apathy; church attendance over Sunday morning recreation; and a spiritual relationship with the Creator over substance use and abuse."[17]

The authors believe that the Million Man March may mark an important milestone in the history of the black struggle for equality in the United States. As a call from within for regeneration and responsibility, it could represent an important maturing in the black struggle.

V. Taking the Steps Needed for Empowerment

The last thirty years have been a period of great progress in the pursuit of equality and at the same time a period of disappointing failures. The problem is complex and its solution evasive. The battle must continue, and it must be waged on all fronts — social, political, and economic. An essential need is to build and improve black institutions, and five of the most critical are the church, education, political involvement, job preparedness, and entrepreneurship.

The black church is one of the few existing institutions that can easily be built upon, for it has a long history of service to its people.

Education is a different matter. Most public schools for poor children are inferior and difficult to improve. It is inconceivable that there are so few great major black colleges and universities, especially when you consider that 90 percent of black U.S. college graduates over 45 years of age graduated from a black institution. Many more young people must be convinced that the pursuit of academic excellence is important in the quest to pursue economic power for themselves and their people.

A great need is for political institutions that will work to get a high percent of black people in this country go to the polls.

Mechanisms are needed which help blacks to be fully employed and to move up the ladder in the major corporations of America, and this does not mean one token black. Black representation on major boards in America is of great importance.

Business ownership is the traditional route to empowerment in the United States. Institution-building in this area should aim for the complete range of enterprises, including newspapers, radio stations, television stations, automobile dealerships, manufacturing plants, and sports franchises. Where blacks are unable to own large businesses, they must become major stockholders.

Total and effective involvement in the national agenda is critical. The time when Africentrism was a meaningful option has passed. Black Americans must stand together, but there can be no question that, at the highest level, unity within rather than separation from the larger society is essential.

A window of opportunity exists, and it is a critical time in the black struggle. Cornel West, widely respected black history professor at Harvard, says that the African-American community is at a transitional moment.[18] We agree.

In the material which follows, separate chapters are devoted to the institutions we feel are most central to the empowerment of black America. The book ends with a summary chapter and the outline of a plan which, based on the logic of institutional revitalization and its consequences, can help carry the country forward.

We do not expect the reader to agree with all of our conclusions, of course, but we sincerely hope this book will be provocative and will help to move civil rights back to the forefront of the national agenda.

2

The Role of the Black Church

Where people have been oppressed as a race group, the Church has sought safeguards and concessions for the individual, evading the necessity and responsibility of group action. And while it fixed its eyes on Calvary or kept up an aloofness from political realities, the road has been slipping back under its feet.

EZEKIEL MPHANLELE

The Church among black people has been a social cosmos; it has provided an emotional outlet, a veritable safety valve for people caught up in the whirling storms of life. She has been a source of inspiration and entertainment, of movements and plans which have moved the entire nation.

KELLY MILLER

THE MOST important institution which blacks have built in the United States is the church. It has played a dominant role in the fight for freedom and equality, and it has had an impact on every aspect of African American lives. Contrary to the claim of some who study black history and conclude that the church was an African institution which was resurrected on American soil, the black church is a product of the American environment. The church was always and remains essential to the black future in America.

I. A Brief History of the Black Church

The black church traces its origins to slavery days. One root was in the efforts of the free blacks in the North to escape from their inferior position in white churches and a second root was in what has been aptly called the "invisible institution" on the plantations.

For a time, most planters feared that Christianity would give slaves an egalitarian ideology and a thirst for freedom. Later, slaveowners came to believe that a selective interpretation of the gospel would foster docility and subservience, and they supported a limited form of worship which imitated their own.[1] This did not meet black needs, and a different church developed that very few whites knew anything about, or cared to know about.[2] According to W. E. B. Du Bois, the social dynamics which produced white religious institutions differed radically from those of the black church and its preachers. The black minister appeared early on the plantation, Du Bois said, "and found his function as the healer of the sick, the interpreter of the Unknown, the comforter of the sorrowing, the supernatural avenger of wrong, and the one who rudely but pictur-esquely expressed the longing, disappointment, and resentment of a stolen and oppressed people."[3]

The church gave slaves a way to express their feelings about freedom. Preaching and oratory compensated for proscriptions against teaching slaves to read and write. The church became the center of black life and the "cultural womb" of the black community.[4]

NOT LONG after the end of the Civil War, blacks again found themselves severely separated from social, political, and economic areas of American life, and they turned again to the church for leadership. Most blacks broke formal ties with white denominations, and they continued their development of a different cultural form of expressing Christianity which had its own rituals, oratory, and musical styles. Their worship gave primal consideration to the necessity of freedom as an expression of complete belonging and allegiance to God.[5]

W. E. B. Du Bois says that during the post-Civil War period, the black preacher became more important than in the past. "He was at once a leader, a politician, an orator, a 'boss,' an intriguer, and an idealist. The combination of a certain adroitness with deep-seated earnestness, of tact with consummate ability, gave him his preeminence."[6]

At this time the black church had no challenger as the instigator of culture within the black community and the center of black life, and

homogeneity in its clientele tended to unify. In 1890 about 90 percent of
the black population resided in the South, and more than 80 percent
lived in the rural "black belt" counties.[7]

A process of differentiation among blacks began in the late 19th
century, and it took several forms, including class differentiation, the
development of secular institutions, and the rise of competing black
religious groups.[8] By the last decade of the century, blacks were increasingly dissatisfied with their economic condition and steady erosion of
their rights. Some were active in the Populist movement of the 1890s
which strove for political union among black and white members. The
Populists espoused justice and equality in financial and political areas.[9]

Increasing black ambitions and activism posed a threat to a white
establishment intent on maintaining supremacy. A message whites
found much to their liking was delivered in 1895 at the Cotton States
Exposition in Atlanta by Booker T. Washington, founder of Tuskegee
Institute. Washington told blacks they should accept segregation, and he
argued that they would have to improve themselves financially and
morally before they could be fully involved in the larger society. He
criticized political activity among blacks and agreed with whites that few
blacks were qualified to vote.

Washington, who was born into slavery in 1856, graduated from
Hampton Institute, which was devoted to industrial education. He was
appointed head of Tuskegee Institute in 1881, and under his leadership,
Tuskegee grew from two small frame buildings and 30 students to the
foremost center for vocational training of blacks in the country.[10]

Washington said that, for the time being at least, blacks should
accommodate themselves to their circumstances through agricultural
and industrial training, and he discouraged any other higher education.
He emphasized economic development and support of black business.

Washington's conciliatory and gradualist philosophy was pleasing to
whites, and he became the most famous and influential black leader in
the country. His idea of accommodation was the most widely accepted
view of black-white relations at the end of the century.

AS THE 20th century began, blacks in the South found themselves technically free but living under cruel laws which made them second-class citizens and separated them from opportunities which should have been theirs as Americans. Still, their prevailing attitude was Booker T. Washington's accommodation. He was the recognized national spokesman for his race and was a consultant to President Theodore Roosevelt. Washington retained the support of the great majority of blacks because of his obvious power and the belief that accommodation was the only course possible. It soon became clear, however, that accommodation was not improving the status of blacks in America, and opposition to Washington began to surface. The most prominent opponent was W. E. B. Du Bois, who had supported most of Washington's programs during the 1890s.

Du Bois, a sociologist and historian with a doctorate from Harvard, felt a deep emotional commitment to Africa. He helped arrange a series of Pan-African conferences, the purpose of which was to convince people of African descent of their common interests and their need to work together in the struggle for freedom. Du Bois fought the myths that Africans had made no contribution to world culture and that evidence of African culture had been destroyed during slavery in America.[11]

In *Souls of Black Folk* in 1903, Du Bois denounced Washington for condoning the caste system and for accommodation that "practically accepted the alleged inferiority of the Negro." Rather than meek acceptance of their status, he said, blacks constantly must speak out against oppression and discrimination.

While he agreed that industrial education was important, he put more emphasis on higher education and on the support of black colleges. Du Bois held that the Negro race could be saved only by the "Talented Tenth," the educated minority who were in position to elevate their brothers both culturally and economically.

Du Bois founded the Niagara Movement in 1905 to organize public agitation for constitutional rights of blacks, and he was involved in founding the NAACP in 1909. Washington saw his leadership threatened, and he tried to limit the effectiveness of the NAACP, but he was losing influence because of a growing realization among blacks that protest was necessary.

Du Bois became more militant in time, but his primary aim remained to improve the status of blacks within American society. A different approach was advocated by the more radical Marcus Garvey, who founded the United Negro Improvement Association in 1914. Garvey's ultimate solution was separation as the only way to liberate black Americans from their white oppressors. This would finally be accomplished through wholesale migration to Africa.

Garvey denounced the integrationist, upper-class blacks in the NAACP for being ashamed of their black ancestry and for desiring to amalgamate with whites. He wanted to protect the black masses from the Du Bois-led "cast aristocracy" of college graduates. Garvey dramatized effectively the bitterness and alienation of the black masses, and his radicalism was a precursor to the Nation of Islam and other radical separatist groups.[12]

Washington, Du Bois, and Garvey represent the contrasting positions of accommodation, black awareness and power within the larger society, and separation, positions which have continued to find advocates in the struggle for equality. This split was reflected in the black church. According to Lincoln and Mamiya, a separatist movement in the urban church was one result of the massive migration of blacks from the rural South during the first half of the century.[13]

A study conducted during the 1930s confirmed that there was already a class-oriented difference in the ritual and services of urban churches. Liturgical and deliberative services had evolved to serve middle- and upper-class clientele, while ecstatic services and overt emotionalism served the lower-class and newly arrived migrants.[14]

These differences faded to the background for a time in the mighty battles of the Civil Rights Movement. The struggle by blacks for freedom and opportunity had accelerated after World War II as black soldiers who had fought for their country were not content to return to second-class citizenship. Better economic times and the Democratic Party's decision to make civil rights an issue led to more intensity in the fight and a greater willingness to confront.

A MILESTONE was reached in 1954 with the *Brown* decision of the U.S. Supreme Court. The Civil Rights Movement followed, and in communities across the nation, clergy-led groups agitated and demonstrated for equal social, political, and economic justice. The activism of black rural and urban churches and eloquent and effective leaders like Martin Luther King Jr. energized and unified black America.

The clergy played leadership roles in the Civil Rights Movement because they were generally the best educated among blacks, and they were recognized as community leaders. The black church was at the center of the movement because it was the most viable, long-term black institution and was the heart of community life.

For a time, the drama, intensity, and innate rightness of the Civil Rights Movement produced unity of purpose among African Americans. A great example of common purpose overcoming class differences occurred in Montgomery, Alabama, during the bus boycott of 1955-1956.

Dexter Avenue Baptist Church, whose new pastor was Martin Luther King Jr., was a "high" church attended by professionals and the well-to-do. College football coach Rufus Lewis was identified with the congregation at Dexter, while Pullman porter E. D. Nixon, head of the local NAACP, was a working man identified with the black masses. Both Lewis and Nixon were powerful, well-known leaders in Montgomery, and selecting one to lead the boycott was sure to alienate followers of the other. The problem was solved and unity achieved by selecting King, a young man who had newly arrived in the city, as leader.

Disunity became a bigger problem in the mid-1960s as younger, more radical blacks became disenchanted with the passivism advocated by King and his followers. The resurgence of black ethnicity, new perceptions of self and society, gains in self-respect and self-confidence, and pride in the black power and black consciousness movements reenergized the debate between separatism and inclusion in the larger society.[15]

With the passage of the Voting Rights Bill in 1965, the Civil Rights Movement won its victory, at least in terms of legal rights. This opened the way for the enormous progress of the last 35 years, but ironically, it deepened the split in the black church.

New opportunities in education and employment led to an enormous increase in the black middle class, and those who achieved this status wanted the improved living conditions they could now afford. They moved into better houses and better neighborhoods, and this led to a growing physical and social isolation of the black poor. Churches today reflect this division.

II. The Black Church Today

As the 20th century closes, the black church in America remains one of the key institutions in the struggle for empowerment, and it is called on again to lead all of its people forward. It faces great problems in meeting this challenge because it is not a monolith. Gayraud Wilmore commented that black churches have been the most conservative and at the same time the most radical of institutions. The many elements of the church lack togetherness.[16]

Black pastors and churches have had an increasingly difficult time reaching the hard-core urban poor, the black underclass, which is continuing to grow.[17] The black church in the inner city is in crisis and cannot handle the problems it faces alone. The church as a whole must find a way to address the situation.[18] News on the church's readiness to mount a unified and effective campaign is mixed.

The inner-city church faces strains and challenges brought on by the many social ills of its environment and by apathy. Black psychologist Cornel West speaks of "The murky waters and dread and despair that flood the streets of black America and of debilitating and self-destructive behaviors."[19] Among the array of problems faced in the inner city are crime, violence, substance abuse, deteriorating schools, high populations of homeless and hungry individuals, substandard and insufficient housing, AIDS, deteriorating family structures, high levels of incarceration of young black males, increasing numbers of single-parent households, and a large population of teenage parents. Added to the difficulties is the process of secularization in black communities, which has always meant an erosion in the central importance of the church.

Black inner-city congregations have experienced a creeping decline in membership, and there has been a mass exodus of young men from the church. Among the current generation of young men and boys, an estimated 60 percent have no contact with the church or indeed with any organized religion.[20] Many young black men see turn-the-other-cheek Christian pacifism as irrelevant, some reject Christianity as a faith imposed on slaves, and some are drawn to Islam. A *Christian Century* writer notes that, in the inner city, being a faithful, moral person is against the odds and weight of the entire culture. The black church in the inner city is in crisis.[21]

The black church in general has difficulty finding enough leaders. It is threatened, ironically, because opportunities have opened in previously closed professions. In a segregated society, talented black men and women developed their leadership skills in black churches, and black clergy were among the most highly educated members of the community. This is no longer the case. There is a serious question of whether the ministry of the black church can attract enough of the best and the brightest.[22]

ONLY a third of the black population lives in the inner city, so the problems are not universal. In fact, black churches in middle-class neighborhoods are experiencing dynamic growth. Worshipers gather by the thousands in what have become Christian epicenters of the black middle class. Fueled by the dreams and finances of upwardly mobile blacks, the megachurches offer worship and a range of programs that satisfy spiritual and social needs.[23]

One feature of this success is a return to the unique ritual and style of the past. For a time black congregations emulated the somber style of the white middle-class churches and found themselves losing members. The successful churches now have warm evangelical preaching, systematic Bible study, aggressive social ministries, trained, informed leadership, appropriate staff structures, and efficient management practices.[24]

The largest churches are Baptist and Methodist, and the Baptists always attract the most members. Lacking an organization with a centralized authority and hierarchy, the thousands of independent Baptist congregations have provided a wide field for self-assertion by blacks who desire to become leaders. Membership in individual Baptist churches ranges from less than 50 to as many as 10,000. Total membership in black churches in the United States exceeds 15 million, with more than 35,000 churches. Three Methodist denominations have about two million members in some 12,000 congregations.

Middle-class church success, however, has failed in most cases to extend to the inner city. As blacks move up the social ladder, they tend like their white brothers to desert the Baptist and Methodist churches and seek affiliation with Episcopal, Congregational, Presbyterian, and Catholic churches. Relatively few middle-class blacks have become ministers of Baptist congregations, though the middle-class is represented in the activities of national Baptist conventions. In some cities, Baptist congregations have split along color and class lines, as middle-class members seek to dissociate themselves from the emotional worship of the black masses. Although the majority of the bishops and ministers in the Methodist churches have come up from the masses, they have increasingly adopted a secular outlook toward the world and have given support to middle-class values. A trend has developed for the black middle-class and the urban poor to become more and more separated.[25]

This trend now seems to be reversing to an extent as a growing number of middle-class black churches recognize their larger responsibilities. Black churches are doing such things as organizing parochial schools, establishing feeding centers, creating family life centers, conducting mentoring programs for young black males, erecting and rehabilitating housing, building nursing homes, and developing a spectrum of economic development initiatives.[26] Successful programs at Atlanta's Antioch Baptist Church include drug rehabilitation, operation of a hotel as a homeless shelter, and counseling and assistance to those with AIDS.[27]

EFFORTS to develop a separate black Christian theology extend back more than a century. The reasoning behind this movement is that white Protestant theology is essentially European in outlook. It is culturally conditioned, and no matter how well-meaning its practitioners may be, it cannot identify psychologically with people who are African and who lived under slavery and the Jim Crow system. There is no question that, throughout much of U.S. history, white churches allowed themselves to justify the attitudes and behaviors of their own members and to provide rationalization for discrimination against blacks and others of different racial and social backgrounds.[28]

In 1966, the National Committee of Negro Churchmen (NCNC) published a "Black Power Statement" which held that the time had come for black Christians to make their own interpretation of the gospel and to connect with their African heritage and their contemporary fight for justice. Black theology insists that, in addition to spiritual deliverance, social and economic liberation is part of the gospel.[29] Black Christians have always known that the God of Moses and of Jesus did not create them to be slaves or second-class citizens in North America, says James Cone.[30]

III. Fundamentals for Church Revitalization

One third of black Americans in the inner city live in appalling conditions, and the church which should serve them is weak and in crisis. At the same time, some 40 percent of blacks have climbed into the middle class. Their churches are thriving, with huge memberships and huge budgets. The problems of the inner city can be solved only if the black church as a whole revitalizes itself, regains its identity as the center of black life in America, and takes responsibility for serving all of its people.

The black church must have its own identity. Blacks must establish and identify with their cultural roots; otherwise, they are buying the notion of their own inferiority. At the same time, there is concern about the polarization and divisiveness which could result from too great a separation among Christians. According to black scholar Richard McKinney, a totally separate black theology could result in the substitution of one racism for another.[31]

Martin Luther King said we are all caught in an inescapable web of mutuality. Blacks, whites, and other peoples are together in the United States and must live together peacefully. Certain fundamental human characteristics apply to us all, including the need for love, for feelings of self worth, for close relationships to family, for community, and for self-confidence in the ability to compete and to excel.

James Cone writes that "to love our people does not mean hating whites. Indeed, we cannot love anybody unless we love who we are as blacks, and the culture and history that sustained us through centuries of slavery and second-class citizenship. The enduring message of black power has nothing to do with hate. Rather, black power teaches love. But it teaches us that love, like charity, must begin at home."[32]

There is another reason to reject separatism. Blacks own part of this country. They paid for it with the toil of three hundred years and with blood shed in its wars. It would make no sense to throw away what has been rightly earned.

THE BLACK church in the United States must return to its historic role as the center of black life and of black efforts toward self-fulfillment. The black church, particularly the church of the middle classes, let others take charge of community welfare, says Baltimore attorney Leronia Josey, and "in the process the drugs crept in and the girls got pregnant." Some middle-class black Christians, she says, got too comfortable.[33]

"If we are to build a genuine black future," James Cone argues, "it will take the talented tenth that W.E.B. Du Bois advocated, the mass involvement that Martin King demonstrated, and the integral solidarity with the grassroots that Malcolm X embodied in his life and death. Physical and mental energy, firm discipline, courage and commitment — all these are crucial ingredients for the creation of a new black future. The initiative for the new vision and the creation of the team should come from the black church because it is the only institution with the power and the resources to do the job. The financial resources for the program must come from the black community, with absolutely no help from the white community."[34]

IV. The Church and Morality

The most ancient and basic task of the church is to provide for the spiritual needs of its people and to guide them to higher levels of morality. Urban ghettos today present a moral challenge of the most serious nature, a challenge which stands in the way of the overall progress of Black America.

Gangs are of recent origin as a major problem in the inner city. They developed in their current virulent form in the last 30 years. Ironically, one cause was the opportunity that came to blacks through destruction of the Jim Crow system.

The victories of the 1960s led to higher expectations, and the blind rejection still encountered led to a backlash and to irrational self-destructive behavior. Also, there was a surge of blacks into the middle class, and as several observers have noted, class interests overcame idealism. Those with the most resources separated themselves from the ghetto, leaving the poor to fend for themselves.

Musician Wynton Marsalis believes that these factors led to a break-down in the concept of community that was always one of the strong points in the African American life. "Right now in the African American community," he says, "we have a culture informed by ignorance and vulgarity." Louis Armstrong grew up impoverished, Marsalis notes, and "you never saw him engage in some of the disgusting acts in today's music videos. His statement wasn't, 'Well, I was a victim of prejudice, so screw everything in the world.'" Marsalis says that blacks are tired of seeing garbage elevated and considered the African American way.[35]

Meeting the challenge requires more than pointing out that vulgar acts are wrong, however. It is difficult to reform a prostitute who in many instances makes fifty dollars for 15 minutes' work. Nor is it easy to stop someone from pushing drugs that are accessible and easy to sell. It is the responsibility of the church to convince those persons that what they are doing is not only immoral and illegal, it is self-destructive. If ten percent of those who participate in prostitution and drugs could be convinced to reform, the black community could gain greater racial respect and less crime, and the inner city would be a better place to live.

AMERICA today has the largest teenage pregnancy rate of any country in the "developed" world even though we teach sex education from an early age. Many parents still do not know how to discuss with their children with the overall concept of sex education. They tell their children not to participate in sex. But they fail to say that, while you should not participate in sex until you are a married adult, just in case you do, use birth control pills, diaphragms, and condoms. These should be available at every corner store.

It should be a responsibility of the church to advise every young person in the church — and every young person within ten blocks of the church — that they cannot afford to have illegitimate children. Not only can youth not afford to have illegitimate children, they should not have more children, legitimate or otherwise, than they can afford to educate.

Young people should be apprised of the costs of caring for a child from birth through college. Giving them this information is not difficult because there are many professionals trained to counsel young people in family responsibility. Even non-professionals in this area can be mature and responsible role models and can counsel young people.

Churches must sponsor "male-friendly" activities such as one-on-one mentorships, sports activities, and public discussions. Long-term solutions involve maturing of male self-esteem as well as helping young males view women as equal partners in rebuilding African American families, churches, and communities.

IN 1960, 5.8 million American kids lived in single-parent families. Today, that number has more than tripled, to an astonishing eighteen million. Equally startling is that fact that nearly 40 percent of black children don't live in the same home as their biological father.[36] These grim numbers point to one of the most demanding and urgent of tasks faced by the black church — rebuilding the family.

The family has through the years been a foundation of black life. In *The Strengths of Black Families*, Robert Hill identifies traditional family traits as strong kinship bonds, a strong achievement motivation, a strong religious and spiritual orientation, and a strong work orientation. A sense of extended family traces back to slavery. Family attachments were ignored as slaves were sold, and children were informally "adopted" and raised by other people in their immediate community. The extended family has until recently been a prominent feature of African American family life and has been a major survival tool.[37]

As with other matters, the black community cannot depend on the larger society to solve its problems of family breakdown. Eric Lincoln says that the most crucial of all needs in strengthening the black family is bolstering the personal and cultural identity and the self-esteem of black youngsters, and "these are affected most significantly by the adult role models provided by black churches, both clerical and lay."[38]

Most of all, in plain and simple terms, as a generation of people who are attempting to establish themselves in full equality, blacks must live by the Ten Commandments.

V. The Church and Politics

For blacks to be empowered as a race, the churches must reemphasize responsibilities which are related to the local and national political agenda. A major factor in progress during the last few decades has been black political strength. The involvement of black preachers in civil rights and politics extended a tradition of black preachers serving as social critics and activists.

Important church tasks in political activism include:

- Emphasizing the importance of politics and encouraging members to be involved.

- Assisting with voter registration and promoting voter participation in elections.
- Developing effective political leaders.

The black church has been a powerful influence in politics in locations where blacks have had the right to vote. When blacks migrated to northern cities in the first decades of the 20th century, ministers used their influence over congregations to secure support which blacks had traditionally given the Republican Party. During the Roosevelt and Truman administrations, the black masses shifted their support to the Democrats, who offered a solution to their economic problems, and black ministers were forced to follow the changed outlook of their members.

The important role of the black church was recognized in the struggle to secure the membership of black workers in the unions being organized in the 1930s by the Congress of Industrial Organizations. Managers of the large corporations made contributions and donations to churches in an effort to persuade black workers not to join the unions. Although this was somewhat successful, black workers ultimately learned the role of unions in modern industry through the efforts of a group of liberal black ministers.

STRENGTH in the political world depends directly on the number of votes which will support an issue or a point of view. Voter registration, therefore, is a key to political power in the black community. Every black religious institution in America should be directly involved with voter registration. These institutions should commit their fair share of the cost involved, and they should use their facilities to house persons engaged in increasing minority participation in voting.

The hard job begins after all the work has been done to get the people registered for particular political positions, raising funds within the church to help the candidate financially, and helping to turn out the registered voters.

It is incumbent upon the church to remind members regularly that black people in this country have died for the right to vote. Voting is a sacred thing.

OVER the years, the black church has been the haven for many of the black community's most visionary leaders, from Nat Turner, who led a slave rebellion in 1831, to Oliver Brown, who filed the lawsuit in the 1954 Supreme Court decision, to the leaders of the Civil Rights movement, to Andrew Young who served in Congress and as American Ambassador to the United Nations. These people looked to the church to nurture and build their leadership skills because other institutions of society were closed to them.

Society has become more open in the last 30 years, and blacks now have other opportunities to develop as leaders. This does not negate the importance of the church continuing as a base in leadership development. As the center of black life, the church provides unique prospectives on problems and needs of the black community and on the black political agenda.

VI. The Church and Economic Opportunity

As economist Sylvester Monroe points out, "economics is the key building block of political power."[39] Andrew Young notes that "Investment, education, jobs, economic opportunity, economic justice — these are the weapons we have to employ against the serious threat to our nation posed by poverty."[40] Reverend Cecil Murray adds that, "Spiritual development cannot take place without economic development."[41] The message is to get capital and build wealth.

There is no question that the black community has the potential to build the economic power it needs. What is required is a strategy which connects the necessary people, resources, and institutions and the commitment to carry the strategy through in the long term.

Black business is more important than ever because of the worldwide economic transformation now taking place. Fading fast is the time when a person could work for a single company for years or make a living wage simply through willingness to work hard. People everywhere, of all races and colors, are being thrown more onto their own resources, and starting a successful business is one way to respond and be in control.

A traditional problem blacks have faced is locating the money necessary to go into business, because banks have been reluctant to make loans to them. The answer to this problem is to focus and utilize the enormous financial resources of the black community so that needed funds are available.

THERE are many examples of black churches which promote economic opportunity. Concord Baptist Church of Christ, a 14,000-member church in Brooklyn, built a home for the aged, organized a fully accredited grade school, and developed the Christ Fund, a million-dollar endowment for investing in the Brooklyn community.[42]

In December 1992, as a response to the devastating riots in their city, the First African American Methodist Episcopal Church of Los Angeles launched a Renaissance Program of twenty entrepreneurial projects. Errol Smith, who hosts a black-business talk show in Los Angeles and runs a $5 million custodial company, adds to the case for self-reliance. "You can spend all the money you want on social programs supported by liberals, you can enact all the enterprise zones and tax breaks conservatives might want, and it won't help. Black people need to focus on enterprise."[43]

Housing is a critical area for the inner-city African American population, and it offers an opportunity both for church involvement and for entrepreneurial action. In a beautiful example of broad-scale economic cooperation, five of the nations largest black churches recently announced the creation of a company that will help businesses sell a variety of consumer products and services to congregation members. Part of the profits will be earmarked to help African Americans buy homes. The company, Revelation Corporation of America, is the brainchild of black businessman John B. Lowery of Memphis.[44]

All black churches should be in the financing business to support members who need assistance in starting new businesses and to provide aid and assistance for those already in business. The examples above outline a range of possibilities. Some other things every church can do, regardless of size, are to assure that all church funds are deposited in a black institution and to organize its own savings and loan association.

VII. The Church and Education

Throughout the country's history, quality education has been difficult for most African Americans to obtain. Since slavery days leaders have urged youth to study and to learn all they could. At the same time, denial of education was a tool of the oppressor. It is no accident that the first legal battle in the modern Civil Rights Movement involved education. For all people, education is the key to survival and to prosperity. It is always an essential step on the path to a better future, and it has become more critical than ever because global economies are undergoing fundamental change.

Inner-city schools attended by black students are on average notoriously bad. Their facilities are crumbling, they spend far less per pupil than other schools, and they are beset with violence and lack of discipline. These schools are not prepared to deal with the disadvantaged children who come to them.

Part of the problem is that inner-city children, like other poor children, do not have the background they need when they first enter school. The black church can help alleviate this problem, and those serving poor neighborhoods should have a preschool program as well as accredited kindergarten and elementary programs. Each should provide assistance in helping high school students excel. Children should start at an early age and should be presented from the very beginning of their education experience with high performance expectations. In addition to regular studies from kindergarten to grade six, there must be a programs designed specifically for the slow learner.

The churches should be equipped with libraries sufficient to support the level of excellence intended for their educational program. They should have a full-time librarian if possible. If they cannot afford this, church volunteers should be available every day to teach the children how to use the library.

Computers are very important in church educational programs. They are basic in the new world economy, and they are inexpensive. Many companies would give churches their older computers as a writeoff. Computers have become a way of life and are fundamental, now and in the future, to employment opportunities.

Many churches have begun programs in parenting. They have family responsibility classes, and they teach young men how to be fathers. Some of the programs have been surprisingly successful, with young fathers realizing and accepting for the first time their own responsibility in bringing a child into the world.

The case for church help in providing economic opportunity has been made. In addition to assistance in financial matters, churches need to educate in a range of business and financial practices. Virtually every black church and community organization needs to operate some kind of economic education program, from economic literacy and job training to community loan funds.

VIII. Revitalization of the Inner-City Church

Most examples of successful church programs in this chapter have involved rich churches in middle-class neighborhoods with large memberships. Churches do not have to be large and rich to do significant work in the inner city, however. Inner-city and middle-class churches working together can accomplish great things. This point is demonstrated by Bethel AME church in Birmingham, Alabama. Bethel is the home of Bethel-Ensley Action Task, Inc. (BEAT), an eye-opening success which observers say is reweaving the fabric of the community.

Ensley, where Bethel is located, is a section of Birmingham whose population is 84 percent African American and 16 percent white. The poverty rate for African Americans in Ensley is 35 percent, and almost 40 percent of households are headed by females. Tuxedo Junction, made famous by the 1930s song, is a part of Ensley.

Bethel was a dying inner-city church with a membership of less than 100 when the Reverend Ron Nored became pastor in 1987. The distrust, lack of unity, hopelessness, and despair he encountered forced him to expand his understanding of what it means to have faith, he says, and it strengthened his commitment to a ministry rooted in justice, compassion, and hope.

Nored organized BEAT in 1990, and in less than eight years the organization has built 35 new affordable homes in its neighborhood and will soon add 35 more. Nored brought a number of organizations into the effort, including other congregations which provide labor, funds, and planning help; businesses which donate materials and equipment; and the City of Birmingham which has provided technical assistance, almost $2 million in infrastructure improvement, and financing through housing bond funds.

Young people attend BEAT leadership training workshops which help them make better decisions and change their own lives and communities for the better. BEAT's commercial revitalization program teaches residents how the local economy works, how to do economic planning, and how to carry out economic development activities. It has helped to create several new neighborhood businesses. All of this has given new vibrancy to the church, whose membership has climbed to 250.[45]

Nored says that faith and church "are about transformation and resurrection, not only in the lives of individuals but in entire communities as well. That is why it is so important for churches once again to make redeveloping and building community a priority."[46]

IX. The Church and the Future

As the 21st century approaches, the black church must adopt new ways of thinking about many important issues. At the same time, it must return to its former posture as the social, intellectual, economic, and moral center of the black community. In its revitalization, it must find a unity in purpose which overcomes class differences and allows it to focus resources on those with the greatest need.

Theologian James Cone tells us that, "The ideals of integration and nationalism are insufficient for the problems we now face and for the issues with which we will have to deal in the future. We need to do more than try to be assimilated into white American society or to separate ourselves from it."[47]

Finding this middle ground is more difficult and complex than in the past. Opportunities created through the victories of the 1960s ironically created great complexities. Black America is no longer a single afflicted mass but a multitude of groups beset with class conflicts. The situation calls for strong leadership, and one need is for a new generation of ministers who are schooled in liberation theology and primed not only to preach but to put their beliefs and commitment to work solving problems of those who live in poverty and social disarray. What must be practiced in the future, according to Andrew Young, is a social gospel, with a justice-oriented macroeconomic order, which is inseparable from the Christian faith.[48]

A recent report from the Interdenominational Theological Center points to the need for greater cooperation among inner-city churches and those in more affluent neighborhoods. It also stresses the need for leaders who are trained better in handling financial matters. The report notes that resources available to many black churches to help address the current social and economic problems plaguing poor communities have seriously dwindled. Whether current levels of giving are adequate to answer the call for expanded outreach ministries remains a question.[49]

Black "megachurches" have the funds to finance local social and health programs, but smaller, poorer churches in most cases are unable on their own to increase the community services they now provide. The poorer churches can meet essential needs only if they get help from sister churches in better financial shape.

In the report, Dr. Lawrence N. Jones, former dean of Howard University's School of Divinity, speaks of the need for better-trained leadership: "If African American churches are to remain viable in the years immediately ahead, they will require leadership that is theologically better trained and better equipped with the secular knowledge and skills requisite for dealing with the chronic problems that persist."[50]

At the same time that a new vision is required, it is imperative that the churches of today restore the commitments of yesteryear, when it functioned as an extended family. In this setting things such as character, integrity, and responsibility need to be taught and the audience convinced that they are their brother's keeper.

Early family counseling should be a part of the extended family life. The church should counsel every black child in America on the importance of education, family values, and work ethics. It must convince children that they can perform at the levels of excellence expected of them. The church must also teach parenting and marriage to the family. The powers-that-be in the religious community need to stress over and over that one should first be married and then have children, and not have three or four children and hope one day to get married.

Churches can keep a roster of companies or individuals who employ others on a part-time or full-time basis and can help place those in need in some kind of honorable work. Persons with employment difficulties should be taught prior to going to a job that the most important thing in overcoming their problem is to concentrate on performing better service than they have ever performed before and doing more than what is asked of them. Educational help must be offered to these people.

Black Americans must aim for moral, religious, and economic excellence, and the church has a critical role in this quest. Black Americans must be law abiding. They cannot rob, steal, rape, or do bodily harm to themselves or any other people. Blacks can ill afford to have any black-on-black crimes or black-on-white crimes. A role of the church is to teach nonviolence. This has been one of the concepts that has brought the black community this far.

The extended church family needs to understand that, as a race of people who are attempting to achieve political, economic, and social empowerment for the yet unborn black Americans, they cannot afford to accept handouts or welfare. They must understand that no one is going to do any more for the black community than the black community is willing to do for itself.

3

Education and Black America:
A Glass Half Full

Education consists not only in the sum of what a man knows, or the skill with which he can put this to his own advantage. A man's education must also be measured in terms of the soundness of his judgment of people and things, and in his power to understand and appreciate the needs of his fellow man and to be of service to them. The educated man should be so sensitive to the conditions around him that he makes it his chief endeavor to improve those conditions for the good of all.

KWAME NKRUMAH

The purpose of education is to transmit from one generation to the next the accumulated wisdom and knowledge of the society and to prepare the young people for their future membership in society and active participation in its maintenance and development.

JULIUS NYERERE

BELIEF IN education as an instrument of democracy has long been an article of faith in the United States. Education has been seen as the vehicle of upward mobility, especially for those who are socially and economically disadvantaged. From pre-Civil War days, black leaders struggled to gain more educational opportunity for their people.

It is no accident that the *Brown v Board of Education* decision of the Supreme Court in 1954, which opened the modern Civil Rights Movement, concerned access to quality education.

In recent years, concerns about the quality of education have drawn increasing attention. *A Nation At Risk* in 1983 called attention to the fact that American students were falling behind those of other industrialized countries in math and science. Given changes in the economy, this was presented as a matter of grave concern. It is now seen more clearly that a new emphasis is essential.

Black Americas share these concerns, and in addition face the fact that, for them, education in the United States is a glass half full. One third of the black community resides in the inner city, and as a stubborn symbol of the difficulty of change, educational problems of ghetto children have not improved but have grown steadily worse. In matters educational, a substantial portion of a race is at risk.

I. The State of Education in the U.S.: Good News and Bad

Schools have been a consistent target of the critics of the American scene. The negative assessment is only partially true, for the U.S. has made considerable progress since 1983. A report of the Consortium for Policy Research in Education notes "there are many, many bright spots in the nation's classrooms, and the latest figures from the National Center for Education Statistics show increased performance in recent years,[1] and figures from the National Center for Education Statistics show increased performance in recent years.[2]

The United States has traditionally supported education. In real terms, per-pupil expenditures in the public schools tripled since the 1950s, doubled since the mid-1960s, and rose by about a third during the 1980s. Class sizes have fallen, with the median elementary classroom dropping from 30 students in 1961 to 24 in 1986. The public schools employed six adults for every 100 children in 1960, ten in 1981, and eleven in 1990.[3]

Robert Peterkin, an African American professor at Harvard, adds that "there is cause for at least some celebration in the matter of educating African American youngsters. Steadily increasing percentages of African American students have completed high school," Peterkin continues, "and the achievement gap between white and African American students has narrowed substantially at least with respect to reading and mathematics." "Still," Peterkin observes, "significant gaps remain."[4]

Enrollment figures for preschool children reflect the pros and cons of the national scene. In 1973, the enrollment rate for three- and four-year-olds from low-income families was 15 percent, while that for high-income families was 35 percent. By 1993, the rates for each were 28 percent and 52 percent respectively. While the rate for low-income families increased substantially, the disparity increased from 20 percent to 24 percent.[5]

Education is improving, but change is uneven for different population groups. The system works fine for those with higher incomes and is adequate for the middle class, but its performance is far less acceptable for the poor.

Statistics prove that the value of education to the individual continues to increase:

- In 1980 a college-educated American ten years into his career earned 31 percent more than a contemporary who had finished only high school. By 1988 the earnings gap had increased to 86 percent.[6]
- Between 1980 and 1990, the income of men who were full-time workers with five or more years of college rose by 78 percent compared with 37 percent for high school graduates and 30 percent for those with one to three years of high school.
- Eighty one percent of adults with a bachelor's degree participated in the labor force in 1992 compared with 66 percent of persons who were high school graduates. Labor force participation rates for different racial and ethnic groups were about the same.[7]
- Over the past 30 years, each economic downturn has pushed a larger proportion of the uneducated into unemployment, and each upturn has rescued a smaller proportion of them for the labor market.[8]

The bad news is that major problems remain in the education system in the United States, and they impact most heavily the children with the greatest needs. Among the major problems are violence, noninvolvement of parents, crumbling facilities, and the failure of the nation to move toward greater equity.

VIOLENCE. As we read in the newspapers, violence is growing, and most vulnerable are black and Hispanic youth, who suffer most from poverty and other forms of social neglect. One indicator is the increasing number of kids carrying guns to schools. As a result, children are killing children. An estimated 1.2 million elementary-age children have access to guns in their homes.[9]

An irony is that a small proportion of students cause the problems in schools. Department of Justice data show that most school-age children are law-abiding. Only about six percent of all juveniles are serious habitual violators, but these few are responsible for 62 percent of all offenses and 66 percent of violent offenses.[10]

Joycelyn Elders says that violence occurs because children are learning to use it as the way to solve problems. Violent behavior is modeled for them, Elders notes, in our homes, schools, neighborhoods, and in the media.[11]

PARENTAL NON-INVOLVEMENT. The low involvement of parents in education is critical, especially in the inner city. The breakdown of the African American family unit has been recognized as one cause of black children's failure in schools.[12]

Among the indicators are the increasing number of single-parent households, teenage out-of-wedlock pregnancies, young mothers without parenting skills, young fathers who do not accept the responsibilities of parenthood, schools which have low morale and a shortage of qualified staff, and general social disorganization in inner-city areas.

Studies over many decades, and plain common sense, tell us that the strongest influence on a child's performance in school is the support the child receives at home. The strength of society is inextricably linked to the strength of its families.

CRUMBLING FACILITIES. Crumbling facilities are a serious problem in many areas and are most severe for low-income schools. A recent report of the General Accounting Office, a research arm of Congress, found that many schools nationwide are in substandard condition and need repairs of such things as leaking roofs, toilets, heating systems, storage areas, and structural components such as walls and staircases. The GAO report notes that schools with inadequate buildings are likely to be the least prepared for 21st century technology needs, and it estimates that $112 billion is needed to bring all facilities to minimum standards.[13]

EQUITY. The disparity between the educational opportunities of rich and poor may be the most serious problem now confronting the American educational system. Despite years of effort to help low-income students, progress has not been sufficient. There is great danger, in fact, that this problem will get worse.

Allan Odden notes the ironic situation of property-poor, low-spending districts often being geographically close to rich, high-spending districts. This puts in bold relief the "systemic inequity that has long plagued the fairness of the American educational system."[14] Census Bureau figures show that the income disparity between the poorest and richest is rising and is the largest it has been since the end of World War II. It is sobering to note that:

- Forty-four percent of African American children live in poverty.[15]
- Only 58 percent of preschoolers (aged three to kindergarten entry) with household incomes under $10,000 attend any type of preschool program, as compared to 79 percent of preschoolers with household incomes over $30,000.[16]
- With the move to a global economy, the risk of underemployment and unemployability has intensified for the most vulnerable youth.

In the 1980s, realization that funding had consistently risen while achievement remained flat led to the conclusion by many that education had a significant productivity problem. Intense pressure grew both to improve education quality and to reform school finance structures.

The Bush administration reacted with an Education Summit in 1989. After the summit, Bush and every governor pledged to launch a comprehensive approach to education reform. Goals 2000 was the resulting program. Planning began under President Bush and continued in the next administration. The enabling legislation was signed by President Clinton on March 31, 1994. The Act passed with large majorities in both houses of Congress.

The National Education Goals associated with the program state, among other things, that by the year 2000, all children in America will start school ready to learn; all students will demonstrate competency in English, mathematics, science, foreign languages, civics, economics, history, and geography; every adult will be literate and possess the knowledge and skills needed for a global economy; and every school will be free of drugs, alcohol, violence, and unauthorized firearms and will offer a disciplined environment conducive to learning.[17]

A critical question is whether these efforts at reform go far enough. Critics agree among themselves that a minimum strategy must include specific student performance objectives, flatter organizational structures, major decision-making by those actually providing services to students, and strict accountability for results. This approach requires a level of decentralization not previously attempted, and it depends on strong financial support at the very time education finance is in turmoil.[18]

II. Education and the Global Economy

Profound economic and social changes are occurring throughout the world in the closing years of the 20th century. They are driven by advances in computer technology and telecommunications. As a result, great changes in job requirements and related skills are occurring.

According to the U.S. Office of Education, many Americans are not equipped with the academic and occupational skills that the increasingly complex job market requires. American students and educators need awareness of the knowledge and skills that the workplace will demand of them, but what we have instead are vague feelings of insecurity as layoffs occur and the newspapers carry stories of downsizing.[19]

The At-Risk Youth Task Force states that job demands will make grade fourteen (high school plus two years of college) the minimal educational level for successful employment. "Most entrants into the labor market of the 1990s and beyond," the report concludes, "will require a higher educational level than ever before in the nation's history."[20]

It is clear, say Michael Weisburg and Eldon Ullmer, that an educated person will be someone who, in addition to basic skills, will have "learned how to learn" and be prepared to continue learning throughout a lifetime. The notion of education as a formal process occurring at a specific location during a fixed time frame will not meet the requirements of the next century.[21]

The way we run schools now may have worked in an industrial economy when people settled into career paths from which they seldom veered and when only a small elite needed a solid higher education. This will not keep the country competitive in the 21st century.

One of the needed changes may be something akin to the old apprentice system. The 14-year education requirement does not necessarily imply college. For students who are not college bound, it may involve a cooperative effort between business, industry, and education, and it can consist of a combination of on-the-job activity and classwork. The training will, of course, focus more on lifelong learning and flexibility than similar efforts in the past.

A GREAT danger to the nation in this environment is the growing disparity between rich and poor. It is more important than ever that solid preparation for learning begin when children are very young. People must understand at a young age what the job market is like and what their own personal stake is. Unless they are set on the right track early, it will be more difficult than in the past for them to recover as they grow older.

Manufacturing and service jobs will remain, of course, but they are a continuously decreasing segment of the job market. This means that there are more "at-risk" people competing for them and that, consequently, wages for these kinds of jobs are falling. A generation of young people face underemployment or unemployment.

Commentator Peter J. Paris notes that, "America is no longer dependent on a black laboring class. To the larger society, blacks are dispensable in an economic sense. The black masses, the majority who have not made it yet to the middle class, can no longer depend on the crumbs from somebody else's table." To this majority, Paris points out, education is not just vital, it is the key to survival.[39]

Blacks and Hispanics will account for more than one-fourth of all entrants to the labor force between 1990 and 2005. As Angela Webster notes, "Large segments of the African American community are neither educated enough to fully participate in building a high-technology economy, nor are they wealthy enough to participate in consuming its products. This vast community remains high on the list of the education-ally at-risk."[22]

The changing economy and conditions in the inner city interact to make equity in education a critical issue. We stand in great danger of creating a permanent underclass, encompassing at least five percent of the total population, which is without a real stake in the society, without hope, and likely as a result to resort to violence and lawlessness.

III. General Issues in Education

Until the late 1950s, the federal government's role in education was limited. A step toward more involvement was taken in 1958 when, in response to the launch of Sputnik by the Soviet Union, Congress passed the National Defense Education Act. The big increase in the federal role came in 1965 with the Elementary and Secondary Act (ESEA). Despite continuing Republican efforts to reduce federal involvement, a signifi-cant federal presence has continued.

The federal role in education remains a sharply debated issue, with elimination of the U.S. Department of Education a goal of the political right. Federal involvement is an issue on which the Democratic and Republican parties have sharp philosophical differences.

There appears to be consensus that two programs which give aid to poor children, Chapter 1 (originally Title I of ESEA) and Head Start, have succeeded and should be continued, even though the rightwing has attacked both. Otherwise, a sharp debate on reducing the federal role in education continues. Such a reduction would, of course, mean a great increase in local decision authority and local financial responsibility.

SCHOOL FINANCE is in an unsettled state because of taxpayer revolts, the general shift to the right in the political climate, uncertainties related to the economy, and the demand for school productivity. In several states, property taxes, long the basic component of school finance, are being reexamined, and a shift to some type of sales tax is contemplated.

No matter what financial system is adopted, the problem of unequal expenditures seems to persist. Between 1966 and 1989 annual per pupil expenditures in constant 1989-90 dollars increased from about $1,900 to $4,700 nationally. But the increase was not proportional. For example, in 1990 the 100 wealthiest districts in Texas spent $7,233 per pupil while the 100 poorest districts spent only $2,978.[23] Poor schools continue to have fewer resources in spite of court rulings that expenditures must be equalized

Advocates of reform call for local management of the school and classroom through teams of teachers and parents. This can only work when information, knowledge, budget authority, and authority over personnel and rewards are decentralized. Exercising local budget power in this way would require redesign of teacher compensation, and this is another explosive issue.

Many reformers, such as Chester Finn, contend that finance and other problems can be reduced by giving consumers a choice of the education they will receive and the institution from which it will be obtained. They argue that freedom in selection and the resulting competition to supply services will increase the quality of the product. This, they claim, will result in greater benefits for amounts spend.

This idea may have merit when consumers are well-informed and have the background and experience to make decisions. Poor and uneducated consumers, however, often lack the needed knowledge and understanding. Choices in education are complex. The powerful idea of individualizing is based on matching educational experiences to the needs of the individual learner, and this requires a high level of relevant information.

Decentralization and increased choices are strong ideas, but they need to be tempered for those in poverty. Just making a range of high-quality alternatives available and then leaving everyone to sink or swim on their own is not likely to solve the problems of equity. It might even make them worse.

SINCE the late 1950s, major programs with lofty goals have been announced periodically. Some improvements have resulted, but the education system continues in essentially the same form it had before Sputnik, with the exception that the federal role increased significantly during the Great Society era.

Given the global economy and the pressing need to address equity more effectively, the time may have come to do more than patch up the old system and use new names for old practices. If systemic changes are needed, they must be in sufficient depth to make large differences, and history proves this will be very difficult.

Finn maintains that the strategies for change must include a major shift of authority and control from producers to consumers. This, he says, entails cracking the establishment monopoly. He maintains that a further requirement is accountability mechanisms which have real consequences for everybody involved, including classroom teachers.[24]

Robert Peterkin says that smaller facilities are needed. This approach is being tried in Chicago, New York, and Philadelphia, which he calls the nation's three centers of effort at improvement for the disadvantaged. The effort involves school-based management and mini-high schools of choice created by small teams of teachers.[25]

Some of these ideas involve radical restructuring and require that real power be reallocated. A question is whether change to this extent is necessary and, if so, how such groups as the American Federation of Teacher and National Education Association can be persuaded to go along.

Broad agreement is expressed that standards should be higher and should state specific levels of student performance on specific tasks. A related need is to assess the extent to which objectives are met and to use results for accountability and for designing corrective steps, but an unresolved question is how a school or school system should carry out the required assessment. Testing is a difficult, highly technical problem, and informal teacher-made tests will not suffice. Even if an individual district had the financial resources and the technical expertise, the development of suitable tests would still be a problem because results in one locale must be comparable to those in another. Otherwise there is no way to evaluate progress relative to other districts, states, and countries.

School professionals, including teachers and administrators, are like other workers in the new economy in that they must be prepared for lifetime learning and for regular adoption of new ideas and practices. This requires expanding the meaning of professional development. Reformers increasingly recognize that traditional staff development, with one-shot workshops, is incompatible with current needs.[26]

Significant changes at higher education level are also needed. Educators and policymakers working on reform have become increasingly critical of colleges and universities for lagging behind the times. Higher education has impeded reform, they say, by failing to get its own house in order.[27]

A PROBLEM always for poor people is their lack of leverage to influence decisions. In theory, democracy gives everyone an equal say in government, but in fact, as we all know, it doesn't work that way. This is true both because power naturally follows wealth and because the poor tend to be uneducated and lack the knowledge of how to participate in political processes.

The idea of placing power in the hands of consumers, as it is elsewhere in the free-enterprise system, has great appeal, but it could still leave the poor at a disadvantage. Unless a way is found to give real power to all of the stakeholders, the reinvented system will work like the old. It will be great for the wealthy, adequate for those in the middle, and ineffective for those on the bottom.

Needed changes may require fundamental restructuring and are large in any event. They are certain to be strongly opposed by those who now exercise power in the educational system. The NEA and AFT, principals and superintendents, other employee groups, state and local school boards, textbook and test publishers, and colleges of education all have an interest in things remaining the same. The needed change will be impossible unless understanding and consensus can be developed among the public and a high level of political will developed. To this stage, policy makers, educators, and analysts have found it difficult to explain the systemic nature of their proposals, and public skepticism remains high.

IV. Special Concerns of the Black Community

The issues discussed above are relevant to all citizens. Other matters are more pertinent to African Americans.

Over 100 years ago, Frederick Douglas wrote, "If we are ever elevated, our elevation will have been accomplished through our own instrumentality." Earlier this century, W. E. B. DuBois remarked in a similar vein that progress by blacks would depend on themselves. DuBois said that through education African Americans would move throughout the larger society and "would use their knowledge and skills in economics, in social policy, in public administration, and in political theory and practice" to help their brothers. Shirley Thornton, executive director of the San Francisco Housing Authority, notes that, "Today's black middle class has in fact exceeded DuBois's prophecy in terms of educational and economic gains."[28]

The Consortium for Policy Research in Education presents evidence that gaps in achievement between African American and white students have been substantially reduced. Between 1970 and 1988, the percentage of African American parents of elementary school aged children who had completed 12 or more years of schooling increased from 36 to 69 percent.[29]

But major problems remain. For example:

- Almost two-thirds of African American students remain in predominantly minority schools, and nearly one-third remain in almost entirely segregated schools.[30]

- Although African Americans comprise less than 15 percent of the high-school population, they represent 50 percent of all dropouts nationwide.
- The unemployment rate among African American males is the highest of any population group.
- As a group, African Americans score lower than other students on academic achievement tests.[31]
- Secondary schools with large proportions of minority and low-income students offer few advanced courses and have smaller academic and larger vocational programs than other schools.[32]

Conditions in the inner city leave large groups of youth "at risk." These young people are less likely to accept the beliefs of previous generations and more likely to feel disconnected from mainstream culture and behavior. Many have replaced church, school, and family socialization with a dependence on peer influence. Such problems place these youth at great risk of chronic unemployment, crime, and drug addiction.

ACCORDING to Courtland Lee, the literature in recent years has referred to young black inner-city males as an "endangered species." "From an early age," Lee says, "black males are confronted with a series of obstacles in their attempts to attain academic, career, and personal-social success." Lee quotes these indicators:

- Mean achievement scores for black male students are low in basic subject areas.
- Black males are much more likely to be placed in classes for the educable mentally retarded and for students with learning disabilities than in gifted and talented classes.
- Black males are suspended from school more frequently and for longer periods of time than other student groups.
- Black females complete high school at higher rates than black males.[33]

"The stark fact," says Franklyn Jenifer, "is that we are losing African American males all along the education pipeline." At Howard University in the fall of 1991, only 33.8 percent of the undergraduate enrollment and only 27.7 percent of graduate enrollment were African American males. Jenifer further notes that a growing number of black males are unequipped to be adequate breadwinners, husbands, and fathers. "This threatens the viability of the black family," he says, "and beyond that, the progress of African Americans as a people.[34]

Black adult role models are critical in addressing the situations. Social, cultural, and economic forces often combine to keep young black men from assuming traditional masculine roles, Courtland Lee contends, and he makes the cogent assertion that "only a black man can model the attitudes and behaviors of successful black manhood."[35]

Black males who drop out of school are, of course, much more likely than others to find themselves in trouble with the law. To society at large this matter has great relevance even if one only considers its financial aspects. The yearly costs of incarcerating an individual are much higher than the costs of sending him to college.

Contributing to the difficulty is a severe shortage of black male educators in American schools. It is not unusual for a black boy to go thorough an entire school career and have little interaction with a black male teacher, counselor, or administrator. The number of minority teachers is shrinking. At one time, black teachers comprised 18 percent of the U.S. teaching force. Today, fewer than seven percent of teachers are black, and that number is projected to be less than five percent in a short time. The reasons are very complex.

The problem is caused in part by success of African Americans in entering other careers. In 1966, education was chosen by 23 percent of black college students and was the most popular major. By 1978, only 6.8 percent were education majors. Education now competes with other fields, such as law, business, medicine, and engineering, and the stature of teaching has diminished.

Moves which might help alleviate the situation include early identification in school of likely candidates; improved guidance; strengthening historically black institutions of higher education; recruitment from diverse sources such as the armed forces, community colleges, adults desiring mid-career changes, and school paraprofessionals; and, an essential, decent salaries.[36]

In a guest editorial in the *Journal of Negro Education*, Franklyn G. Jenifer, president of Howard University, said that "Many African American males find themselves caught between the 'rock' of educational attainment and the 'hard place' of job qualification." A chief reason, Jenifer noted, is "the impact of the shift in the American economy from one based on manufacturing to one based on technology and service."

Jenifer continued, "The days when you could make it up the economic ladder without education, through hard work — through jobs that relied more on hard physical labor rather than sophisticated knowledge and skills — are going fast."[37]

Jenifer's remarks reemphasize the danger of the global economy producing greater inequities, and they stress the great threat the situation poses to youth, particularly males, in the inner city and other poverty settings.

FOR THE black community to be successful in education in the next several years, it must set high goals for its children. It should expect that children in the first years of their schooling will:

1. Read and write beyond grade level.
2. Study a foreign language in the elementary grades.
3. Develop an operating knowledge of computers early in the school experience.
4. Study music and play at least one musical instrument.
5. Learn about several great artists and many great books.

Lest one supposes that these goals are too high, remember that expectations are of critical importance. If by word or deed you tell kids they can't succeed, they won't, says Stanford psychologist Claude Steele, who has conducted extensive research on this matter. Over time, Steele maintains, "stereotype vulnerability" can cause students to stop identifying with achievement in school.[40]

Reverend Buster Soaries of the First Baptist Church of Lincoln Gardens, Somerset, New Jersey, reminds us that children must be motivated to learn. "You could give a school a billion dollars, and if the children are not motivated to learn, or are embarrassed to do well, it won't do any good," he says. We have to build a climate of high expectations and of success.[41] Educators have long known that self-concept can lead to self-fulfilling prophecies, that what a person believes he or she can accomplish can be a determinant of what actually can be done.

Shirley Thornton stated in a 1994 address at Howard University, "We must attack one of the main reasons for our present-day problems: our ongoing feelings of inferiority." "People who love themselves," she said, "seek to preserve their lives, not destroy them."[38]

PERHAPS the greatest challenge to the African American community today is unity. A larger proportion of blacks are making it to the middle class than ever before, but once there, many want nothing to do with the problems of the poor.

Today's black middle class has not lived up to DuBois's vision of applying the tools, talents, and resources of economic success to build a bridge between themselves and the black underclass. Atlanta school superintendent Jerome Harris says, "When I look around at middle-class black people I am reminded of the saying, 'We have met the enemy and he is us.'"[39]

According to Clarence Hughes, the unique history of African Americans, with its episodes of chattel slavery and of cultural and psychological discontinuity, make it difficult for blacks to reach a unified position on several matters related to American society at large. Some African Americans favor the infusion of ancient African values and knowledge forms in society and oppose cultural assimilation. Others believe in self-help, in economic empowerment and self-sufficiency and consider ancient African values irrelevant. Still others hold that the larger society is responsible for centuries of social disorganization and should provide compensation.[40]

However this may be, the fact remains that the ghetto threatens the day-to-day existence and the future of a full third of black America. The problems there, poverty, ignorance, lack of educational opportunity, and cultural confusion and disorganization, were produced in large part by a history of discrimination and racism. African Americans have made astounding progress in the last thirty years. They have enormously more economic and political power than they had at the end of the civil rights era. It is essential now that they find the unity through which they can lift the less fortunate from hopelessness and despair.

V. Effective Change in Inner-City Education

The country cannot allow problems of equity to grow more serious if it is to face successfully the challenges of the global economy. Inner-city and other poverty schools must be brought into the broad mainstream.

Studies prove that it is possible to create learning environments in inner-city schools in which students achieve at levels well above average. Necessities in achieving this are to cut dropouts and provide a rich, culturally relevant learning environment. Dropouts are three and a half times more likely to be arrested and six times more likely to become unmarried parents than those who graduate.[41] Further, they obviously do not meet the 14-year education minimum requirement for job security in the global economy.

The course of study must provide students with rich and varied experiences which lead to college or to a meaningful school-to-work transition program. This requires linkages between secondary and postsecondary schools, business, government, and unions. On the matter of cultural relevance, many inner-city youth report, with considerable logic, that they consider the instruction offered at "regular" schools irrelevant. Among other things, a culturally relevant environment enables students to develop a sense of control.[42]

WHAT would a model program for inner city schools be like? While we do not claim special insight into the problems nor special facility for dealing with them, we are convinced that careful review of the literature reveals features which can help significantly. We are also convinced that trying to force inner-city youngsters into what is now the normal pattern of schooling will not succeed in making them productive citizens.

Features we believe are necessary are:

1. Major organizational restructuring with smaller facilities and decentralized decisions. In the inner-city setting, at least, we come down on the side of radical change. The current system simply is not working. Decentralization requires strong leadership at school level. It also requires valid assessment to indicate how students, teachers, and the schools are doing. Overcrowded situations in large buildings are an invitation to trouble. Changing to smaller facilities is sure to be controversial, however, because of the investment in existing structures.

2. Parent involvement in general decisions about school operation and in decisions about their children. Joyce Epstein, co-director of the Center on Families, Communities, Schools, and Children's Learning at Johns Hopkins University and a leading expert on parental involvement in education, says that most parents want to help, but they don't know how. She and her staff have identified several types of information and training which assist parents in effective involvement. Topics include parenting skills, ways of creating supportive learning environments at home, effective communication with school staff, volunteering for parent help activities, and leadership skills. This type of program addresses the need discussed earlier of helping parents from poverty areas make informed choices on complex educational matters.[43]

3. Early intervention. To do well in their formal education experience, students must be prepared in their preschool years. This is an educational truism which has proved difficult to address in poverty areas. Success is possible, however, as demonstrated by the High/Scope

Perry Preschool Program. This is an early childhood program with substantial outreach to parents. One fourth of the nation's Head Start programs use some or all elements of the related curriculum. Cost analysis showed that the program returned $7.16 for every dollar invested. The program empowers children by encouraging them to initiate and carry out their own learning activities, and it empowers parents by involving them as full partners with teachers in supporting their children's development.[44]

4. Physically attractive facilities with a rich, orderly learning environment. Among other things, this means control of violence. Jerome Harris, Superintendent of the Atlanta Public Schools, states that learning can only occur in a safe and orderly environment. The key, Harris says, which is missing in most schools, is a clear policy regarding violence and disorder, a set of procedures for dealing with specific situations, and training which informs managers and teachers what to do when particular problems occur.[45] The question of rights is sometimes raised with regard to disruptive students. All young people have the right to the best education possible in our country. In the case of a few violent offenders disrupting the educational opportunities of the majority of students, however, there is no question that habitual serious offenders must be removed from regular classrooms.

5. Black male teachers who can teach and serve as counselors. Young black males need specific guidance to master educational challenges, and black male teachers and counselors can handle the task most effectively. Guidance they receive should foster responsible behavior, provide opportunities to analyze the image of black men, expose them to black male role models, and develop a sense of cultural and historical pride in the accomplishments of black men.

6. Significant community involvement, with active participation by black businessmen and other successful black people. In addition to increasing the number of black male educators, other ways must be found to ensure the presence of black males in the classroom. Community representatives might serve as tutors, educational assistants, storytellers, "room fathers," and field trip escorts. The need for black

males to interact with successful businessmen, sports figures, and other leaders has been widely discussed in the literature.

7. Curriculum focus on communication, science, mathematics and other basics and on extensive use of computers and information technology. Such a curriculum must have high standards and high expectations for student performance, and it must be clearly designed to prepare students for a future in the global economy

8. A real stake in the future. Students in inner-city schools must perceive that they have a stake in the future of the country and in the chances of their own success. There must be meaningful incentives to perform well individually. Students cannot be hoodwinked, and this feature is dependent on the larger society making the incentives and promises real and not an empty hope.

9. Finance. The first essential for such an ambitious program is sufficient funding. Almost 40 years after the *Brown* decision, the disparity in school spending between black and white students is in many parts of the country greater than before the decision.[46] Per pupil spending, the physical resources of the buildings, and support for teachers' salaries may not assure better schooling, but they are a necessary condition without which improved learning is not possible.

A VERY innovative and promising program for involvement of inner-city parents has been developed in Buffalo, New York. The school board there rents, for a nominal fee, a large space from the Urban League. The center has a large open space ringed on three sides by conference rooms. Part of the space contains 60 computers, with headphones for those who cannot read well. The computers are used both by students and their parents and can be checked out and taken home.

Another large room is used for kindergarten children and contains a variety of toys, books, and blackboards. On one side is a room with a one-way mirror so parents can watch their children interact with professionals. The center sponsors workshops for parents in everything from computer training to crafts.

Parents are referred to the center or recruited from lists provided by schools, and transportation is offered from various points in the city. Some parents use the center as a place to watch their children do homework. Some are primarily interested in the computers. Others read to their children from the center's collection of books.[47]

VI. A Time for Rededication and Commitment

As the 21st century approaches, a major worldwide economic shift, similar in scope to the Industrial Revolution, is occurring. The interests of black America are more than ever intertwined with those of American society at large; King's reminder that we are in this life together is now more literally true than ever. At the same time, black Americans are more than ever dependent on unity, responsibility, and self-sufficiency within.

At a broad level, the keys for the black community are the same as for the society at large: lifelong learning, adult literacy, knowledge and skills for the global economy, and the background required for responsible citizenship.

A truth which must be internalized by black America and by the larger society is that the most effective way to improve education for poor children is to increase the income of parents. Children from poverty-stricken families will always be at a disadvantage, and providing opportunities for them will be more difficult, no matter how well-intentioned or well-planned the effort, than for children who have strong support systems in place.

Franklyn Jenifer reminds us that there are no quick Band-aid solutions. "We must invest in quality preschool education," he says. "We must invest in quality K-12 education. We must ensure that every youngster has a home environment that is conducive to learning, and when this is not the case we must consider strategies such as residential schools and mentorship programs. We must invest in postsecondary vocational training for young men and women who are not college bound. For young people who want to go on to a four-year college and beyond, we must ensure that resources are available which allow them to obtain such education regardless of their ability to pay, as long as they are prepared to work hard and to pay back any money they have borrowed."[48]

As Jenifer points out, job training for inner-city youth can be very important in the short term in providing them an avenue to escape the street culture. Self-destructive behavior often results from hopelessness, and preaching to someone that their behavior is immoral is not the cure. Youth caught in this situation must have a real way out through decent jobs and better places to live.

EDUCATION is a commitment. We are convinced that every individual in America who is committed to an educational program for themselves, their family and their children can obtain most of their goals and objectives.

Some of us are not qualified to be doctors, engineers or rocket scientists. But we are qualified to obtain education in other fields. This does not mean that one should have a degree from a two-year institution or a four-year institution. It does mean that one has raised his or her capabilities beyond the ordinary. Being a good painters helper requires a form of education. Being a good sales clerk takes a form of education, and so does being a good hamburger maker.

When foreigners come to our country with a language barrier and overcome this obstacle and set every type of academic record, the question is why can't we black Americans? We cannot because we are not committed. If we were, we would limit television viewing to two hours a day and restrict it largely to educational news. We would make sure our children have a complete electronic information system that supplies them with material gathered around the world, even if this means giving up other things we want. As a people, blacks cannot afford not to be educated, and it is imperative that black Americans move to the front in preparation for the global economy. They cannot afford to come in second.

The older generation tells us they studied by candlelight, walked five miles to school in all types of weather, had a one-room schoolhouse with one book and one teacher for five grades, and they didn't turn out too badly. They suggest that a similar approach should suffice today. This is the same logic as driving a T-model Ford on a German autobahn. We must make available all the educational technology for the yet unborn black generation. African Americans must summon the will, courage, and unity to carry on with a struggle which is only half finished.

4

Involvement in the Political Arena

No one has earned the right to do less than his best. Kennedy defeated Nixon by twelve thousand votes in 1960, Nixon defeated Humphrey by five hundred and fifty thousand votes in 1968. Carter defeated Ford by one million and seven votes in 1976. One fourth of the total black vote is between the ages of eighteen and twenty-four; there are more registered black young people alone tonight than the cumulative margin of victory in these national elections over the past two decades; we must use it and not abuse it and fight to get our rights and our freedom.

REVEREND JESSE JACKSON

Politicians are necessary, and it'd be foolish to blame them for our troubles. They're just doing what they have always done — looking to survive, looking to climb, trying to please everyone at once and grinning and lying while they're doing it.

RAY CHARLES

T HE LAST thirty years have seen a great struggle for Black America to take its rightful place at the political bargaining table. How does the struggle stand as the country nears a new century?

This question goes beyond voting to the matter of individuals and groups getting their fair share of the fruits of the political process. Voting is necessary, of course, but it must translate into the more expansive concept of political empowerment, which might be defined as equal opportunity to influence political decisions at all levels of governmental activity.

Success has been mixed. With the Civil Rights Act of 1964 and the Voting Rights Act of 1965, all legal barriers to black empowerment were removed. Under the protective eye of the federal government, the new era began with great progress. Certain elements of the majority culture, intent on protecting past privilege, sought to limit black political influence, however. Attempts were crude at first but in time were evolved into a very sophisticated strategy we call the "Reagan/Bush White Counter-Revolution."

In general, progress toward black empowerment was substantial from 1965 to 1980, but it slowed to a crawl after Reagan became President. In fact, the next twelve years saw determined attempts to beat back what had been accomplished.

The Clinton Presidency gives hope that the era of regression is over. Whether this is true is the key political consideration as the nation approaches a new century. Is the United States now ready to resume its quest for political equality and fairness?

I. Progress Since the Voting Rights Act

In the years following passage of the Voting Rights Act in 1965, there was an extraordinary integration of the races, a striking expansion of the black middle class, and a powerful contribution of blacks to mainstream culture. Within a decade, black voter registration climbed by more than 1.5 million to a total of more than 3.5 million in the eleven states of the old Confederacy. By 1980, more than two thousand blacks held elective office in the South, compared with fewer than one hundred before the passage of the Voting Rights Act.[1] American society was in a transformation which, it seemed, could transcend the racial problems of the past.

Beginning with the victories of Carl Stokes in Cleveland, Ohio, and Richard Hatcher in Gary, Indiana, African Americans were elected to the mayoral office in a large number of American cities. However, the majority of these were in cities with large black populations in racially polarized elections. Because few garnered large percentages of white support, it was believed that blacks and whites voted almost solely on the basis of racial identity and refused to cast crossover votes.

Currently, there are about 7,000 elected African American officials in the 50 state and local governments, and there are 40 black members of

Congress. If appointed positions are included, some 15,000 blacks now hold office.[2]

SIGNS of white reaction appeared almost immediately after the Voting Rights bill was signed. Black registration quickly went from five percent to 50 percent of eligible voters in the next five years, but white registration increased sharply during the same period, thus negating, in absolute numbers, the black voters added to the rolls.

Beginning with the Nixon administration, Republicans attempted to slow progress toward black political empowerment and to undo steps that had been taken. Nixon was only partially successful, partly because he found himself embroiled in the Watergate affair.

By the time Reagan took office in 1981, however, strategies had been worked through and the national electorate had taken enough of a turn rightward for a partially successful counter-revolution to be mounted.

Many white workers who were in the middle class salary-wise but who held blue-collar jobs defected from the Democratic party. They were greatly threatened by affirmative action and by programs which used quotas to give blacks greater employment opportunities. In their own eyes, their jobs were at risk, and they were the ones being asked to pay the price for past discrimination. They became Republicans or "Reagan Democrats" and supported a new "conservative egalitarianism" which was opposed to special preferences for blacks, unions, or any other liberal interest.[3]

Reagan's strategy played on a mix of race, big government, and white working-class anger, and action ranged from assaults on labor to a broad attempt to dismantle the civil-rights regulatory structure to efforts to overturn court rulings favoring minorities. Among other things, Reagan appointed several new conservative members to the Supreme Court and prompted a turn rightward in its civil-rights decisions.

The assault continued under President Bush. The racial nature of his approach was perhaps best illustrated by the Willie Horton incident during the 1988 election. Horton, a black "career criminal," was depicted in a series of commercials by the Bush campaign in an attempt to show that Democratic nominee Michael Dukakis was soft on crime. The commercials were widely viewed as racist in character.

Progress toward black political empowerment slowed, some progress of the past was reversed, the judicial system became more conservative, and perhaps worst of all, the electorate became polarized with blacks and whites suspicious of each other and at odds rather than cooperative.

The Christian right became an important part of the effort to roll back civil rights progress as it energized itself politically during the Reagan/Bush years. It seems strange that people would attempt to deny other human beings their dignity and rights in the name of a religion based on love, compassion, and caring for one's neighbor; it seems strange, that is, until the rationalizations of slavery and segregation by certain groups of white Christians are recalled.

The Christian right has used many strategies of the Civil Rights Movement successfully as it has energized people, given them strong convictions of moral correctness, and motivated them to register and vote. It has been very successful in getting people elected locally, and it was part of the driving force behind the Republican's Contract with America success in 1994. The Christian right has gained great influence in the Republican Party, and while it does not have the numbers to dictate party positions, it exercises effective veto power over candidates and platforms.

Everything the Christian Right has done is legal, and it has been so effective that those of us who do not agree with its message have to look on with grudging admiration. It is succeeding through good organization, commitment, and hard work. The only way to counter such an effort is through better organization, greater commitment, and willingness to work harder.

Unfortunately, inner-city problems were compounded as the country turned right. Racial progress ran into such roadblocks as crime, welfare, dependence, illegitimacy, drug abuse, and a generation of young men and women unwilling either to stay in school or to take on menial labor. Some 30 percent of the black population found itself caught in this situation of social dysfunction.

As Henry Louis Gates, director of Harvard's Afro-American Studies Department, concludes, "Despite all of the progress, nothing is more paradoxical that the fact that today we have the both the largest Black middle class and the largest lower class in history." He calls the situation of Americans blacks today both "the best of times and the worst of times."[4]

The major task now, for black America and for the nation at large, is to address the inner-city problem at the same time that other advances are consolidated. This could not be done effectively under the divisiveness of the Reagan/Bush Counter-Revolution. We believe that the reelection of Clinton in 1996 and the 1998 midterm elections mark a turn from the right and a new commitment in this country to achieving racial fairness. This in turn supports the assertion that Black America, for the first time in the nation's history, is at the threshold of full political empowerment.

II. Some Current Challenges and Realities

One of the greatest challenges to African Americans is to avoid what Guinier calls "The Tyranny of the Majority." According to the Census Bureau, as of July 1, 1996, the national population was 73.3 percent white, 12.7 percent black, 10.5 percent Hispanic, 3.4 percent Asian, and 0.1 percent other. The numbers make clear that racial polarization, a continuing thrust of Republican tactics, must be avoided. As Stephen L. Carter states it, we must "preserve a vision of America that almost nobody really believes in but almost everybody desperately wants to. In this vision, we are united in a common enterprise and governed by common consent."[5]

This is easier said than done, of course, and it brings up some difficult issues, such as how do you avoid color consciousness at the same time you are trying to protect group interests? How do you make sure that black candidates are elected if you do not vote as a group and support them?

Several other challenges and needs are relevant, including voter participation, court rulings against gerrymandering, race and class, keeping losers involved, the matter of a mainstream or separatist outlook, and dangers in one-party voting.

CENSUS Bureau figures give a startling history of black voter participation in the years since the Voting Rights Act of 1965 was passed.

Percent of Registered Black and White Voters
Who Have Voted in Federal Elections Since 1965

Year	Total	White	Black
1966	55.4	57.0	41.7
1968	67.8	69.1	57.6
1970	54.6	56.0	43.5
1972	63.0	64.5	52.1
1974	44.7	46.3	33.8
1976	59.2	60.9	48.7
1978	45.9	47.3	37.2
1980	59.2	60.9	50.5
1982	48.5	49.9	43.0
1984	59.9	61.4	55.8
1986	46.0	47.0	43.2
1988	57.4	59.1	51.5
1990	45.0	46.7	39.2
1992	61.3	63.6	54.0
1994	45.0	47.3	37.1

In all 15 federal elections since the passage of the Voting Rights Bill, the percent of registered blacks who voted has been less than the percent of registered whites.

In the seven Presidential elections, the average percent of blacks who voted was 53.6, while that of whites was 63.8. In non-Presidential years, the average percent of blacks was 39.8 and of whites was 49.7. Overall in the 15 elections, the black average was 36.7, and the white average was 46.7. The numbers were closest in 1986, when 43.2 percent of registered blacks and 47.0 percent of registered whites voted.

This raises an unavoidable question: How do African Americans expect to be taken seriously and have an impact on political decisions in this country if they don't bother to vote in greater numbers than these?

Registration among blacks is also a problem in that about five percent fewer eligible black citizens register than whites. Daniels points out that there are still approximately eight million African Americans unregistered to vote in the U.S., including some 430,000 in Florida; 500,000 in Georgia; 420,000 in North Carolina; and more than 1,000,000 in the state of New York.[6]

Addressing this problem is a key step in the empowerment process. The potential power of the black vote was demonstrated in the 1998 midterm elections in which Democrats nationally won a surprising victory. The election results left no doubt that black voters can have a major impact on political outcomes in the United States. Analysts reported that African Americans turned out in higher-than-usual numbers nationwide and played a significant role in the Republican defeat. Blacks helped Democrats to victory in Alabama, Georgia, South Carolina, and Georgia, showing that the Democratic party is alive and well in the South.[7]

Only about 37 percent of eligible voters in the total population voted in 1998, and the average for the last four midterm elections has been less than 40 percent. Even though blacks comprise only about 13 percent of the national population, they can make their power felt by voting in larger proportions than the total population, a tactic followed by the Christian Coalition and conservative right.

The impact of minority voting was demonstrated both in Texas and Florida in 1998. George Bush, Jr., appealed to and won the Hispanic vote in Texas with what has been called a smiling, compassionate conservative, and he was reelected by a landslide. Jeb Bush won the governorship of Florida with the same approach. When he ran and lost two years earlier, he said, "nothing," when asked what he would do for blacks. In 1998 he had specific answers to the question, and with an increase in black support, he won.

The results prove that black Americans have it in their power to play an influential role in the political process and in doing so to protect their interests and to help determine the political agenda. This message should sink deep into the consciousness: blacks have substantial political power, but to exercise that power they must register and vote.

As part of its rightward swing, the Supreme Court is reviewing congressional seats which are "reserved" for blacks. It recently held that a Georgia congressional district was unconstitutionally drawn because it attempted to maximize the number of African Americans in the district to increase the chances that an African American would be elected. The ruling held that, for a redistricting plan to survive, it must be narrowly drawn to achieve a "compelling government interest."[8]

Just what constitutes a compelling government interest is not always clear. What is clear is that the practice of assuring there will be black office holders through redrawing election-district boundaries is under heavy attack and is being scaled back. The point has been made that empowerment is not necessarily assured by having blacks in office, but the opposite is also certain. There will be no empowerment without black office holders.

Without special election districts, the alternative seems to be that black candidates must have broad appeal and must win on merit among the larger voter population. Recent results support the notion that, if blacks vote in sufficient numbers, this can happen.

THE matter of whether to play politics in the mainstream or to be deliberately separatist is still a primary issue, at least among black intellectuals. Henry Louis Gates represents what has been called "pragmatic multiculturalism" a position close to integration with the mainstream.[9] Gates recognizes that blacks are in many respects more conservative than whites on social issues, and he contends that African Americans need a "politics whose first mission isn't the reinforcement of the idea of a black America." Gates says it is now time for "cultural glasnost" on the race question.[10]

The separatist point of view concerns itself with black ambivalence about American citizenship and is characterized by expressions of rage and pain for past and perceived present injustices. Its prime architect is said to be Temple University Professor Molefi Asante.[11]

In our view, separatism is not the answer. There must be group consciousness, unity, and concerted efforts to increase black voting and black empowerment, but the only course which can bring about desired results in the long term is to do these things within the context of the larger system.

Some 82 percent of blacks remain Democrats and vote accordingly. This figure raises the question of how someone expects to exert leverage if they always vote the same way. Can African Americans as a minority group afford the luxury of being identified with a particular party? As things stand, the Democratic Party can often take black votes for granted, without any commitment to black interests.

It seems obvious that black Americans could gain leverage if the single-party identification were eliminated. To make this possible, however, Republicans must make a more effective attempt to appeal to blacks. As long as they engage in divisive, race-bating tactics that are designed to polarize, they make voting for anyone but a Democrat extremely difficult.

III. Strategies to Achieve Empowerment

Given the opportunity for the African American community to proceed to fuller political empowerment at this time, and given the current situation nationally and related challenges and realities, what are some strategies for achieving the desired outcome? The literature and experience suggest several.

First, there is no question of the absolute necessity for organization, dedication, intense effort, and the continuation of aggressive advocacy.

The religious right gives the perfect example of a relatively small proportion of the population exerting great influence on the political process. This group, led by such stalwarts as Jerry Falwell, Pat Robertson, and Pat Buchanan, began their effort several years ago to move the

Republican Party to their way of thinking about social issues and the proper role of government. At the same time, they openly advised their followers in churches to vote Republican, and they maximized their influence by delivering the vote.

They've irritated many a Democrat by succeeding and making themselves the most powerful religious force in politics today. They did it through raw effort — through getting themselves organized, getting fellow believers actively involved, working long and hard, and voting in elections.

Robert Heineman notes one of the reasons why such an effort can succeed:

> Within a context of widespread indifference from much of the community, public officials will face organized, intense groups who are unwilling to compromise and who are accomplished at political tactics. In the face of these efforts, local officials may find it impossible to maintain a semblance of general welfare in their decisions or to provide functional protections for the rights of the less organized and less articulate portions of the community.[12]

In other words, large numbers of people are indifferent, and if you will work hard for your cause, you will get attention and almost certainly achieve some of the results you want.

THE three-day African-American Leadership Summit hosted by the NAACP in Baltimore from June 12-14, 1994, was the most diverse and perhaps the most important single gathering of black leaders in 20 years. Everyone attending the summit recognized the political necessity of coalition politics.

Lenora Fulani stated as a matter of principle that, "We share a common understanding that black unity is based simultaneously on the black experience and on living in America. As people of African descent living in America, the issue isn't whether or not we work with white folks. White America is all around us. The issue is which white folks we work with and what the objectives and terms of coalitions with them must be."[13]

With less than 13 percent of the national population, African Americans have no choice but to make coalition building a matter of first importance. The major issue for black candidates seeking to organize a viable winning coalition is uniting with groups with parallel interests. It goes without saying that such alliances must carefully balance the interests of all coalition members,

Sharon Wright in the *Journal of Black Studies* points out that there are many benefits to be gained from coalitions in addition to simply increasing numbers. These include financial support from the white middle-class community plus increased and at times more favorable media converge.[14]

A deliberate ploy in the Republican counter-revolution strategy has been racial divisiveness and polarization. This caused many observers to conclude that racial polarization was a permanent part of the political landscape in the United States. The November 1989 elections proved that such assumptions on the inevitability of racially polarized voting were false. African American candidates won mayoral elections by attracting large levels of white support in cities that lacked black majorities, including New York City, New Haven, Seattle, Cleveland, and Durham. Also, L. Douglas Wilder was elected as the first black governor of Virginia. These candidates ignored racial issues in favor of those that were common concerns of both minority and white voters.

A large proportion of black candidates in the past campaigned on issues of primary importance to black voters, and after winning, they acted as though black voters and their concerns were their total constituency. This is understandable perhaps, but it is polarizing. As the creation of special election districts gives way and there are fewer districts with a majority of black voters, candidates must find ways to generate broader appeal. They have no choice but to follow the examples of Douglas Wilder and of the successful mayoralty candidates.

During much of the past 30 years, political campaigns which involved competing interests of black and white population elements were treated as though a zero-sum game were involved. The conception was that the side which received at least 51 percent of the vote won absolute control and took all of the fruits of the victory. Bitterness and resentment result in such circumstances, and coalition-building becomes very difficult.

Lani Guinier suggests that politics is not necessarily a zero-sum game where the winner takes all. Positive sum solutions, she points out, are far preferable because everybody wins. The idea is that each party with an interest in political outcomes takes is own turn, and each gains in roughly the proportion to which it contributed to the victory. Such a process requires coalition building and trust. It requires open agreements. With a little thought, all parties will realize that this approach increases the probability that all will get at least part of what they want.

As Guinier explains the idea, "Structuring decision-making to allow the minority 'a turn' may be necessary to restore the reciprocity ideal. Giving the minority a turn does not mean the minority gets to rule; what it does mean is that the minority gets to influence decision-making and the majority rules more legitimately."[15]

CAMPAIGNS in urban areas whose inhabitants are largely African Americans require a unified effort and careful organization to assure maximum effect. This is a situation where group action and group unity are desirable. Experience reveals six ideas that will be useful in running campaigns in black urban areas. Many more will surface from time to time.

The six are:

1. The campaign leadership should strongly encourage volunteers and community leaders to engage in as much face-to-face interaction with the black electorate as possible. Face-to-face interaction appears to increase voter turnout among black voters who normally would not vote.
2. Campaign leaders should closely supervise voter contacting activities. Volunteers and community leaders cannot be expected to engage

diligently the voters in face-to-face interaction without the benefit of a carefully developed and closely supervised program. This is a job of the campaign leadership, and it is a tough job that requires a tremendous amount of time and effort. But it must be done if voter contacting is to have its maximum effect on black voter behavior.

3. Whenever possible, campaign leaders should recruit strongly motivated, high-energy individuals to conduct precinct-level campaigning. To be sure, campaign leaders do not have the luxury of dealing only with "strongly motivated" volunteers. Political campaigns will normally use anyone who volunteers. But all too often campaign leaders overlook entire groups of individuals who are likely to be strongly motivated. The recruitment of such individuals should always be viewed as a top campaign priority.

4. Party organizational activity should be conducted in black precincts of all income levels. Party activity has been found to be effective in all types of environments within the black community.

5. Political campaigns should initially concentrate on recruiting community leaders from lower-middle- and low-income black areas to engage in voter contacting activities within those areas. This is not to preclude the recruitment of community leaders from upper-middle-income black areas. But because the average political campaign is quite limited in both time and resources, voter contacting activities should usually be targeted at those areas where they will have the greatest positive benefit.

6. One of the keys in putting a campaign together is to have the finances well structured and organized. It is incumbent upon the political organization to help a candidate with his financial needs and obligations.

AT A MORE fundamental level, Manning Marable, Director of the Institute for Research in African American Studies at Columbia University, writes that the time to base black political strategy and action on race has passed. He proposes what he calls a "transformationist" strategy which makes race potentially irrelevant as a social force.

Marable acknowledges that, "The cultural history of U.S. blacks is, in part, the struggle to maintain their own group's sense of identity, social cohesion, and integrity, in the face of policies which have been designed to deny both their common humanity and particularity. But," he continues, "we must destroy and uproot the language and logic of inferiority and racial inequality, which sees blackness as a permanent caste and whiteness as the eternal symbol of purity, power, and privilege."[16]

Similar ideas appear among several black writers. The principal point is that a move to full empowerment must finally be based on inclusiveness. Trying to be separate and to be part of the mainstream simultaneously is inherently self-contradictory.

IV. The Essential Need for New Leadership

The civil rights revolution of the 1950s and 1960s succeeded in large part through inspired leadership. King was the right man at the right time, a person so rare in his abilities and effectiveness that he won the Noble Peace Prize. He was ably assisted by such unusual men as Andrew Young and Jesse Jackson.

Thirty years later, as the chance to move forward to a new level in civil rights presents itself, the need for strong leadership is as great as ever. A feeling seems to pervade, however, that those currently in the fore are too wedded to the past.

Oscar Coffee, in "Leadership And The Problem," says unequivocally that a new generation of civil rights leaders is needed and current leaders are ineffective because "the role of the black leader has changed."[17] In his book *Race and Responsibility*, Boston University economics professor Glenn C. Loury states flatly that there is a vacuum of genuine black leadership.[18]

Who are the current leaders? As good a list as any is the group which attended the "National Town Hall Meeting" on September 16, 1993, which was sponsored by the Congressional Black Caucus Foundation. Present were Congressman Kwesi Mfume, then Chairman of the Congressional Black Caucus and now NAACP president; Dr. Benjamin Chavis, then Executive Director of the NAACP; Louis Farrakhan; Jesse Jackson; and Congresswoman Maxine Waters from Los Angeles. Perhaps the biggest name missing was Colin Powell.

Many argue that the person in this group with the greatest potential to be a true national leader is Louis Farrakhan. Whether we like him personally or not, Farrakhan speaks for a substantial portion of Black America, and he has a disciplined and effective organization of his own. He cannot be excluded by any sensible coalition-builder.

On several occasions Farrakhan moved himself into position to step up to national leadership, but each time he faltered. Most recently he organized the Million Man March and delivered a message with which few could disagree. More than at any other time, he was poised to take charge. As in the past, however, he followed ill-conceived activities that have ruined his chances.

For example, on October 16, 1996, the first anniversary of the Million Man March, he stood before 100,000 persons at Dag Hammarskjold Plaza in New York and called on the United Nations to "force the United States to atone for murder, violence, and war against African Americans." This was hardly a message of reconciliation.

We can only conclude that within Farrakhan is some weakness that will not allow him to get completely in step with an overall national agenda, and that his potential for leadership will never be fully realized.

All of these people have made outstanding contributions, so what is wrong with their leadership? Critics say that the most serious problem is their continuing tendency to look for salvation from other than within themselves and their community.

In *Race and Responsibility*, Glenn C. Loury discusses what he calls the "ascendent issues of African-American life: the dubious blessing of racial preferences, the dual identity of African Americans, the conflict of racial loyalty and intellectual independence, and the family."[19] Loury is critical of the inclination of black political, intellectual, and religious leaders to blame the "racist American society" for the general condition of the black underclass. Furthermore, he berates the notion that inner-city and poverty problems will miraculously disappear when America finally does right by its black folk.

By focusing on external contributors to the plight of the black underclass, Loury contends, the current leadership has helped erode black communities' historical commitment to self-reliance. "As a result," he says, "we have created an entire generation of black men and women who are convinced they can do little to improve their condition until white America changes."[20]

Closely related to the leadership issue is a "black intellectual renaissance" in the late 20th century. On the morning of the National Town Hall Meeting, a preliminary discussion at Howard University featured four of Black America's most profound intellectuals: Federal Judge Leon Higginbotham, Cornel West of Harvard, Dr. Mary Frances Berry, Director of the Civil Rights Commission, and Professor Lani Guinier, who was short-circuited early in the Clinton administration after nomination as Assistant Attorney General for Civil Rights.

This group represents a flowering in the academic world. According to the magazine *Black Issues in Higher Education*, 102 African American professors currently hold endowed chairs at major universities, more than at any other time in this nation's history.[21]

This group is critical because it provides the intellectual background to conceptualize, plan, and help carry out the next set of empowerment activities. As a concrete example of their contribution, awareness of the debilitating effects of "victim mentality" has been brought to our broad consciousness through the efforts of such academics as Claude and Shelby Steele, Cornel West, and Manning Marable.

If we accept the proposition that new leadership is needed, where is it to be found? The answer is that it probably must be developed among the young. The political education of youth and their motivation for personal involvement thus become essential.

According to Oscar Coffey, young African Americans look to the future without dragging the baggage of past thinking and past solutions. They no longer look to the politics of begging, Coffee says, but search for new solutions.

History tells us that effective leadership must be from within, says Coffee. "We must cast our buckets in our local neighborhoods. We must look at our community as a bastion of opportunity in lieu of a ghetto."[22]

V. The Future: Beyond Race as the Energizing Core

At the beginning of this chapter we stated our belief that Black America, for the first time in the nation's history, is at the threshold of full political empowerment. Realization requires significant change in the political outlook of the two major groups which have been central in the struggle, the majority, which still remains largely white, and African Americans themselves. Our view is that the Clinton Presidency and his smashing reelection in 1996 signaled a change in the population at large.

In the "Foreword" to Lani Guinier's book *The Tyranny of the Majority,* Stephen Carter states that, "Although the nation has problems, some of them caused by racism, we are a people of good will, aiming at a fairer, more integrated society, which we will achieve through the actions of our essentially fair institutions."[23] One could argue that this has not been historically true, but we agree that it is the direction in which the nation is moving. A longer discussion and rationale for this point is given in our final chapter.

As David Bauman observes, at a practical level, changes of this nature require an attitude adjustment by blacks and elimination of a stereotype by other Americans. The attitude and the stereotype are symbolized in the words, "a hand full of gimme and a mouthful of much obliged." The image comes from an old Sonny Stitt jazz blues song called "A Handfulla Gimme," which has these words: "You got a habit even worse than running around, you got a hand full of gimme and a mouthful of much obliged."

That attitude, says Bauman, has become the unfortunate stereotype that marks too much of black-white politics in the United States. Black Americans sprang from a class originally designed to be this society's permanent peons, with strong backs to support the development of the New World. Embedded in black American culture is a stubborn perception that America is a land of oppression rather than a land of opportunity. Both the gimme stereotype and the perception of oppression must change.[24]

In moving toward full political empowerment in the immediate future, we agree with Manning Marable that the nation must replace the bipolar categories and the assumptions of the segregationist past with an approach that is pluralistic, multicultural, and non-exclusionary. We must go beyond black and white and seek power in a world which is increasingly characterized by broad diversity.

But this is not at the cost of forgetting the past. As Marable puts it, "We must go beyond black and white, but never at the price of forgetting the bitter lessons of our collective struggles and history, without failing to appreciate our unique cultural and aesthetic gifts, or lacking an awareness of our common destiny with others of African descent."[25]

LEST WE come across as hopelessly naive optimists, we understand that the move to full empowerment faces difficult obstacles, including substantial numbers of people who do not want it to happen. It will not be easy. We reemphasize that we are discussing potential which may or may not be realized. The task requires all of the strategies discussed above, and it requires dedication, intelligence, sensitivity, careful strategy in building and operating coalitions, and disciplined action.

We know that racism lives and that substantial numbers still hate to the point of violence and killing. This is a small proportion of the American population, but it has the power to disrupt. We also recognize that new black leadership, not yet on the horizon, must emerge.

We end by restating the conviction that, for the first time in American history, full political empowerment of black citizens is possible. We can say with certainty that moving toward this goal will require intense commitment and involvement, at all levels of political action, as it has in the past; it will require a significant increase in voting; and it will require a revitalization of black participation in the political process.

5

Jobs and Employment
in the Global Economy

The American economy is as strong and prosperous as ever. Never before in the history of America have so many new millionaires been created in so short a span of time. But maladjustments have set in. The middle class and the working poor perceive that they have not shared equitably in the fruits of progress and they have sent that message to Washington. We all know that Washington has heard and the demands of the middle class will be met. But what about blacks and the needy poor?

SAMUEL L. MYERS, SR.

We must become mechanics; we must build as well as live in houses; we must make as well as use furniture; we must construct bridges as well as pass over them, before we can properly live or be respected by our fellow man. We need mechanics as well as ministers. We need workers in iron, clay, and leather. We have orators, authors, and other professional men, but these reach only a certain class and get respect from our race in certain select circles.

FREDERICK DOUGLASS

A S THE 21st century approaches, the economic systems of the United States and other countries are in a period of profound transformation. We are moving from a manufacturing base to a knowledge/information industry base, and business activity has broadened from local to global concern. One of the primary institutions in the move to empowerment, the world of work, is deeply affected.

Signs of the change from an industrial- to an information-based economy and from narrow to worldwide concern began appearing some 25 years ago with rapid development of the computer, and momentum picked up through the 1980s. Long-range networking, symbolized by the Internet and the World Wide Web, has now made conducting business on an international scale inexpensive and routine.

"The structure of every industry is changing," Gary Kaplan observes. Markets are global, trade is becoming less obstructed and foreign competition is increasing.[1] International economic dominance by the United States, the pattern since the end of World War II, is being challenged now and will be more strongly challenged in the next century. Business and industry in the United States are facing a new level of international competition, and they must be competitive on a global scale.

An important question is the effect of these changes on the effort of Black America to gain economic and political empowerment. What does the economic shift mean to the black middle class, and what does it mean to the lower class and to those caught in the inner city?

I. The Nature of the Economic Shift

The new era, the post-industrial society, is marked by flexible, information-based technologies and by a decline in the proportion of the work force in large factories and mass production. New market standards in productivity and quality are emerging, as networks allow producers to deliver goods and services anywhere. Succeeding in this environment requires changes in organizational structure and in jobs and related skill needs.

Incomes have risen for persons with relevant background and skills. At the same time, incomes and standards of living for low-skilled workers have been declining. People find themselves changing jobs more often than in the past, and those with the lowest levels of literacy and education, almost half of the work force, are experiencing longer periods of unemployment than other workers.[2]

The manufacturing share of the gross national product has fallen from 29 percent in 1950 to 18 percent today. Only 16 percent of the work force remains in factories.[3] Almost two million manufacturing jobs have disappeared since 1990, adding to the large-scale displacement of workers.

The zenith of the mass production era came in the 1950s. About 500 major corporations owned roughly three-quarters of the nation's industrial assets, accounted for about 40 percent of the nation's corporate profits, and employed a little more than 12 percent of nonfarm workers. These firms have not increased the size of their work force in the last decade.[4]

Manufacturing isn't disappearing. It has, in fact, made a strong comeback from the difficulties of the 1970s and 1980s by adopting advanced automation techniques and reducing drastically the number of workers needed. Instead of manipulating a machine or screwing on parts, the worker now must be able to operate a computer.

At the same time, competition for the low-skill jobs which are available has intensified because the work force has more immigrants, women, and older workers than before. Many displaced workers have had no choice but to take employment in service industries such as sales and automobile maintenance. Of those who moved from manufacturing to the service sector, 20 percent have experienced a decline in pay.[5]

In 1950, 60 percent of all jobs in the nation were unskilled. By 1990, this figure had dwindled to 35 percent, and it is projected to drop to 15 percent by the year 2000.[6]

Success in the high-tech world of international competition depends first on the production of knowledge and second on the ability to use knowledge in developing products and services. Persons who are equipped to operate successfully in this environment are in great demand.

At the other end of the pay scale are the service industries, which are also growing rapidly in number. The U.S. Bureau of the Census identifies such examples as sales; lodging; personal and business services; automotive repair, services, and parking; amusement and recreation; and food preparation and service. While these industries offer opportunities for entrepreneurs, workers in them receive low pay and have little leverage because of the competition for jobs.

Associated with the shift in the economy in the U.S. has been a growing inequality in income between top and bottom wage earners. The inequality grew slowly in the 1970s and more rapidly since 1980.

This reverses a trend which followed the end of World War II. The difference between the income of the top and bottom wage earners fell 7.4 percent from 1947 to 1968. From 1968 to 1994, however, the difference increased to 22.4 percent. High-skilled, trained, and educated workers at the top have experienced real wage gains, while those at the bottom have had real wage losses.[7] On average, having a bachelor's degree doubles a person's annual income.[8]

Economists say that the impact of technology and the split into high-tech and service-sector jobs accounts for the growing income disparity. Adding to these effects are the weakening of unions and the rise of immigration. Union participation is half what it was in the 1950s. Immigrants, who are grateful to fill low-paying jobs, are at their highest number in almost a century.[9]

Between 1980 and 1990, the total population of the United States increased by 9.8 percent. In this period, the African American population increased by 13.2 percent, Hispanics by 53.0 percent, Asians by 107 percent, and American Indians by 38 percent. The major increase in Hispanics and Asians has been through immigration. Foreign-born persons now represent about 9 percent of the population. This compares with a high of 15 percent in 1910 and a low of 5 percent in 1970.[10]

II. Implications for Jobs and Careers

In the past, people assumed that they would spend most of their adult lives working for the same organization. The primary requirements for job security were ability to learn a limited and specific set of tasks, willingness to work hard, reliability, and loyalty.

This comfortable scenario is being replaced with a more competitive, less secure work environment. Job and career patterns are changing rapidly, and new types of planning and preparation are needed for people to assure themselves of a secure economic future. The new framework requires more personal responsibility in developing and maintaining desired skills.

In a new twist, middle-level managers have found themselves out of work along with blue-collar workers. Many layers of middle management have served in the past primarily to receive, process, repackage, and forward information, and machines can now perform these functions more efficiently and at less cost than people can perform them. As a consequence, organizational structures are being flattened.

Another trend is farming out many functions previously performed within the organization, a process called "out-sourcing." There is a growing reliance on small external enterprises which function loosely in production networks and pay lower wages, and as a result, jobs within the organization are eliminated.[11] This trend has attracted the wrath of unions, but to little avail. A positive side is increased opportunities for entrepreneurs, which will be discussed in more detail in the next chapter.

According to a recent study of the Labor Department's Department of Labor Statistics, employment during the first decade of the 21st century will be affected in the following way.

Projections for types of jobs:

- Sixty percent of today's high-school students will work at jobs that do not currently exist.
- Manufacturing's share of total jobs is expected to continue declining, with a projected decrease of 350,000 jobs. Manufacturing will maintain its share of total output through increases in productivity. It will account for 12 percent of employment in the year 2000. Manufacturing jobs will be in short supply.
- Four out of five jobs will be service-related.
- Health services, business services, social services, and engineering, management, and related services are expected to account for almost one of every two wage- and salary-earner jobs added to the economy.
- Professional occupations will increase the fastest and add 4.8 million jobs, the most of any group. In contrast, jobs for service workers are expected to increase by 3.8 million. These two groups, on opposite ends of the educational and earnings spectrum, will provide 46 percent of total job growth over the period.
- Other groups projected to grow faster than average are executive,

administrative, and managerial occupations; technicians and related support occupations; and marketing and sales occupations.

- Administrative support occupations, including clerical, will grow much slower than average over the period and slower than they have in the past, reflecting the increasing impact of office automation.

Projections for the labor force:

- The portion of labor force age 45-64 will grow faster than that of any other age group as the baby-boom generation continues to age. The labor force 25 to 34 years of age is projected to decline by almost three million, reflecting the decrease in births in the late 1960s and early 1970s.
- Participation of women in nearly all age groups of the labor force are projected to increase, but at a more moderate rate than in the last ten years. Labor force participation rates for men are projected to continue to decline for all age groups under 45 years of age. As a result, women's share of the total labor force will increase to 47 percent.
- Asian and Hispanic segments of the labor force are projected to increase by 41 and 36 percent respectively, the black component will grow by 14 percent, and the white component by 9 percent.
- By 2006, the black and Hispanic labor forces will be nearly equal in size.

Projections for education and skills required:

- 90 percent of all jobs after the year 2000 will require knowledge of computers.
- Growth rates over the 2000-2006 period will range from seven percent for occupations generally requiring vocational training to 25 percent for occupations requiring a bachelor's degree. Jobs that require an associate degree or more will grow faster than the 14 percent average for all occupations.
- 85 percent of jobs will not require a four-year baccalaureate degree.

They will, however, require interpersonal skills, computer literacy, and a strong basic skills background.

The report adds that the best employment opportunities will be in the Sun Belt and the West Coast, which are the fastest growing parts of the country. The best states for new jobs in these regions are North Carolina, Tennessee, Georgia, Florida, Texas, Arizona, Colorado, and California.[12]

THE NEW framework makes extensive use of what has been termed the "knowledge worker." Labor experts predict that, by the close of the decade, 44 percent of workers in the United States will be in the business of collecting, analyzing, synthesizing, storing, and retrieving information.[13] Generally, these workers require extensive formal education and the ability to locate and apply different types of knowledge.

Compared to workers of the past, knowledge workers require a broader set of skills. They need "flexibility, problem-solving and decision-making ability, adaptability, creative thinking, self-motivation, and the capacity for reflection." Because much middle-management will be eliminated, knowledge workers must be able to grasp the whole context of a problem, and they must take more responsibility for seeking solutions than they have in the past.[14] They may even be able to work at home part of the time. Almost half of U.S. households now have a personal computer, and advances in networking make it possible to work from any location.[15]

Displaced workers who are not highly educated and who do not have the needed skills to fit in some way in the world of knowledge workers have little choice but to take jobs in the lower-paying service industry. According to Willard Daggett, unskilled workers will become structurally unemployable by the 21st century.[16] The situation of these workers presents a growing moral issue to the nation. While individual businesses and industries must be lean and adaptable to survive in a climate of intense international competition, the nation cannot allow a substantial group of its citizens simply to be abandoned.

The only realistic option is to "retread" as many of them as possible, so to speak, and make it possible for them to be productive. This requires special educational and training initiatives, the exact nature of which is uncertain. A major challenge, therefore, is preparing displaced workers for jobs that will let them achieve a higher standard of living.

III. Implications for Education

In the 1992-1993 period, fewer than 10 percent of adult men with four or more years of college were victims of a low-wage employment shift, while the rate for those with a high-school education or less was 30 percent. Of the 3.1 million full-time, full-period jobholders in 1992-1993 who had low wages for more than 13 months, 77.9 percent were workers with high-school education or less.[17]

More than just traditional education and technological training are essential, however. The successful worker in the new context must be adept at interpersonal communication and able to elicit cooperation with other people who are needed to perform part of a task, and these skills have not traditionally been considered primary educational goals.

The demands of the new economy require that grade fourteen (high school plus two years of college) be the minimal educational level for entrance into the labor market, and students must also learn how to access knowledge, a skill restricted almost entirely in the past to graduate-level education.[18] In the new, rapidly changing environment, knowledge can quickly lose its value. Furthermore, its volume can be so great that it is very difficult to find exactly what is needed. The worker with a comprehensive grasp of the computerized knowledge system and how to access it is in demand.

Subjects which are important today and which were not traditionally taught in high school and the first two years of college include statistics, logic, probability, measurement systems, technical writing, technical reading, and applied physics.[19] To meet new demands, more high-school graduates must enter and complete a four-year college education. The far greater challenge, however, is to address the needs of those not bound for a four-year college. Currently, fewer than half of high-school graduates start college, and only about a third actually receive a degree.[20]

Three promising models for building bridges from school to work have been suggested. These are youth apprenticeship, career academies, and cooperative education. All of these require business as a major player, and they involve community colleges in a pivotal role. Other needs are career guidance and counseling for all students, school-based learning integrated with worksite learning, and preparing students for further learning.

One of the most promising ideas is apprenticeships which involve a partnership between schools and businesses. One successful program exposes students in grades 8-10 to information about various occupations, offers 10th graders a choice between pursuing an apprenticeship or remaining in a purely academic track, and creates a three-year apprenticeship starting in grade 11. Students spend at least 75 percent of the third year of apprenticeship on the job.[21]

Junior colleges have an important role to play in building bridges to the world of work for students who are not college bound. Most will need to redefine their mission, however, and revamp their curricular efforts.

Major trends in reshaping curricula in two-year colleges include shifts in emphasis from teaching to learning, from the college degree as a terminal point to learning as a lifelong activity, and from emphasis on a national economy to a global economy.[22]

Skill requirements for the knowledge-based, high-technology era change quickly, and as a result, specialty knowledge becomes obsolete in a relative short time. In the new economy, post-formal education and re-schooling must become a way of life, and people must understand this reality. At present, only 16 percent of U.S. workers receive company-sponsored training to keep their skills up to date, and very few take outside courses of any kind.[23]

THE U.S. has long had the best higher education system in the world but has recently fallen behind other countries at the K-12 level. We concluded earlier that the K-12 system is outstanding for the privileged, adequate for those in the middle-income range, and a disaster for the poor. For the good of the country in the new highly competitive international scene, this casual attitude toward the educational well-being of a substantial portion of the population cannot be allowed to continue. Work force development is no longer an optional investment. The quality of the work force is the foundation of the new economy and the lifeline to the future. The United States can no longer afford to waste human resources.

As *Business Week* recently wrote, the return on investment in human capital is now higher than the payoff on physical capital investment.[24] This is a point that business and industry, plus the large moderate middle of the electorate, need to recognize and internalize.

The United States is the international leader in knowledge industries because of its higher-education system and the research it has done since World War II. Recently, as demands for balancing the budget and cutting expenditures have increased, Congress and governmental agencies have shown a willingness to cut research funding. This could be a fatal error.

Other nations are preparing strenuously to compete. The European Union has been working ten years to produce an economic unit as large as the United States, and it is succeeding. Nations on the western side of the Pacific Rim are progressing rapidly in technological competency, and China is emerging as an economic (and military) superpower. Our continued leadership in knowledge production is not assured and will come under stern test.

Fierce economic competition between nations and blocs of nations will be a feature of the 21st century. This has major educational implications for individuals, and it has broader implications for societies. It would help no one, black or white, if this country should slip to second-rate status or worse. It would, in fact, be disastrous to the job and career prospects of a substantial portion of our citizens. It is imperative that the U.S. maintain its position as the world's leading knowledge producer.

IV. Societal Effects

"I'm mad as hell, and I'm not going to take it any more!" The sentiment was expressed over and over during interviews in the 1994 elections. It represented a widespread feeling that something is wrong in our system.

Yet, the people being interviewed could not articulate the nature of the problem. After the statement, "I'm not going to take it any more," interviewers would sometimes ask, "What is it you are not going to take anymore?" The respondent would stumble and finally answer with a broad generality like, "What those people in Washington are doing." If probed, they could not be more specific.

Feelings of unease were widespread, but the specific reasons behind them were vague. Observers who studied the problem concluded that the major cause was insecurity about changes in the workplace. Large numbers of layoffs were occurring, and workers who thought they were fixed for life found themselves searching for work, often in lower-paying jobs. People sensed that the work place is less secure than at any time since the Great Depression.

Changes in the economic system are similar in scope to the move 150 years ago from an agrarian to an industrialized society. As sociologist Seymour Martin Lipset notes, periods of rapid occupational change produce destabilization and unrest in society. Class structure, the level of job satisfaction, changes in income and life styles, and political issues are all affected.[25]

In the early stages of such a period, demands for different types of education and for different employment patterns are placed on social institutions shaped by the conditions of an earlier era. At first, the performance of these institutions is unequal to the task, leading to greater unrest. Eventually, relevant institutions and the underlying values of the culture evolve to suit the new conditions.

An ominous side effect can be that people who perceive themselves as threatened are more likely to seek scapegoats and to be aggressive in trying to protect jobs. Civility can give way to defensiveness, bigotry, and contempt. Another effect of the economic shift has been a split of large segments of the population into high and low wage groups, as noted earlier. Concurrently, the portion of the population in the middle class has been gradually diminishing. The result is the loss of a comfortable lifestyle for millions of Americans. The United States is in danger of losing the mediating effect of a large middle class, which has been a primary source of stability.

At the same time, a structural "underclass" of citizens, which appears to be permanent, is growing. The underclass consists of less-skilled, less-educated workers who find themselves either unemployed or mired in low income with little opportunity for upward mobility.

It is too early to predict long-term effects. There is no question, however, that the changes have undermined traditional culture, religion, and family ties, and in many cases have produced a less favorable attitude toward work and employers.[26] There is clearly the potential for growing class conflict and for a society which is less stable than in the past.

V. Threats to the Quest For Full Empowerment

The global economic shift poses a threat to the position of blacks in American society and to their chances for continued advancement. The message of hope which is an underlying theme of this book is based in part on the fact that, in the fifty years since World War II, the economic position of African Americans has improved faster than for any other group in American history. Approximately 40 percent of American blacks rose into the middle class during this period.[27] Full empowerment in the society depends on the economic power of a strong black middle class.

Data show that, as the information age advances and the gap between the rich and poor widens, blacks are hurt relatively more than other segments of society. The unemployment rate among African Americans is still about twice as high as that of the nation as a whole, and downsizing in corporate America has hit black executives relatively harder than their white counterparts.[28]

The black middle class is particularly vulnerable. Large numbers of blacks moved into blue-collar, unionized, mass-production jobs which paid middle-class and upper-middle-class wages, but these were jobs which did not require advanced education nor special technological skills. These are precisely the jobs that are disappearing the fastest.[29]

Part of the problem is that the black middle class is narrowly based. Relatively few African Americans have advanced into the professions, such as law and medicine, which are less vulnerable to economic change. Blacks are also under-represented in specialties which require high technical skills, and they are significantly under-represented as entrepreneurs and business owners.

In 1992, African Americans occupied only seven percent of managerial and professional jobs in the country. A Labor Department report showed that African Americans comprised two percent of architects, three percent of physicians, under four percent of engineers, and three percent of lawyers. They held 9.5 percent of the technical specialty jobs which require high-level skills and which pay high wages.[30]

At the very time that increases in managerial and professional jobs need to increase, the enrollment of blacks in postsecondary education appears to have suffered a precipitous decline in the last few years.[31] This runs counter to the impressive advances of African Americans in lower levels of education, a trend in place since World War II. Over the past 25 years, minority proficiency levels in math, science, and reasoning skills have improved significantly. In 1940, only 1.3 percent of blacks were college graduates. By 1970, this figure had increased to 4.4 percent. It was 8.4 percent in 1980, and had grown to an impressive 11.8 percent in 1989. Since 1989, it has remained at about 11 percent.[32] The fear now is that this increase will stop and even reverse itself.

Black psychologist Claude Steele notes another sign that the danger of a fall-back in education may be real. Figures he has gathered show that 70 percent of all black Americans at four-year colleges drop out. This compares with 45 percent of whites.[33] While the reasons for this difference are not totally understood, it is alarming and must be addressed.

African American workers are critically under-represented in con-

tinuing education and job training, especially in formal training supported by employers. Blacks make up approximately 10 percent of the
American work force, but they receive only about five percent of the
formal work force training.[34]

A key question is whether these figures in fact represent the beginning
of a trend. If they do, they signal a danger which must be addressed
quickly, for such a trend would develop at precisely the time that the
need for education is gaining in importance.

We have previously cited Gates's observation that there is today both
the largest black middle class and the largest lower class in history. The
black lower class is, of course, concentrated in the ghettos of the nation's
larger cities. An essential requirement for blacks to advance out of the
ghetto is the availability of meaningful long-lasting jobs. Yet, census
figures show that, in recent years, blacks have been much more likely to
fall back into poverty than whites and to have more difficulty recovering.
The median duration of periods in poverty during 1992 and 1993 was
6.2 months for blacks and 4.6 months for whites.[35]

The Reagan/Bush white counter-revolution succeeded in producing
a backlash against many affirmative action programs. Job losses, cuts in
social programs, and the replacement of community and collective
interests with self-interest have worsened the situation among inner-city
blacks.

The nature of inner-city problems — low educational attainment
and limited opportunities, high unemployment levels, high violence and
crime rates, and general social dysfunction — makes residents there
extremely vulnerable to current economic shifts. They may be the most
vulnerable population group in the nation, and changing economic
conditions threaten to make addressing their problems more difficult.

THE KEY concern of this chapter is the effect of the economic shift on
the effort of Black America to move to economic and political empowerment. This may be a time of hope and potential, but to repeat an
essential point, it is a long way from hope to fulfillment.

The great progress of the last 30 years is encouraging and proves that the goal of full equality is achievable. Black America now enjoys enormously more economic and political power than every before. Current changes in the economy and in the job market, however, assure that the next steps will be just as difficult and the problems faced even more complex than in the past, and they will require the same level of dedication and determination that gave produced progress before. Some actions which are needed include:

- Keep pressure on the system. Recent incidents with Texaco and with an Avis dealership in North Carolina make this need clear. Andrew Young put the situation in perspective when he noted that the behavior of Texaco executives was the norm for almost every big company in 1965. The fact that it received so much publicity and is so distasteful today is evidence of the distance the country has traveled. At the same time, Young emphasized, the situation proves that big changes must still be made. Everybody in this country, in public and private organizations, must understand that Texaco-type insensitive, racist behavior is simply not acceptable at this time and will not be tolerated. Jesse Jackson was correct in calling national attention to what happened and in calling for a boycott. Whenever such an event occurs, officials must be exposed to the glare of publicity, and they must understand that such behavior is not allowable in American society today.

- Make improving education the first priority. At this point in history, the only way to get into the high-tech, knowledge-based world and avoid being trapped in the underclass is through education. More than ever before, equal employment opportunity for all citizens revolves around education. The education system of the United States is generally a disaster for the poor, and this situation cannot be allowed to continue. Significant improvement is essential, and billions of dollars may be required to bring to adequacy educational facilities used by the poor. Public understanding will have to be developed for such expenditures to be politically feasible.

- Reemphasize black unity. Unity is as critical as it has ever been, but it must be unity within the larger system. Errol Smith notes that, in the current setting of globalization, black separatism will retard, not advance, the progress of African Americans. It "excludes us from participation in the newly evolving networks and alliances upon which the new global community is being built," Smith says. "Any inability internally to build strategic alliances across racial and ethnic boundaries ultimately makes our entire nation less competitive in the international marketplace," Smith notes. "For African Americans, in particular, a commitment to black separatism is tantamount to political and economic self-marginalization."[36]

- Greater individual initiative is essential. The move toward economic empowerment must involve as large a portion of the black population as possible, and an essential is establishing firmly the concept of individual responsibility and initiative as the first requirement for success. As Birmingham Mayor Richard Arrington, writers Alan Keys and Glen Lowry, psychologists Claude and Shelby Steele, Andrew Young, and other black leaders emphasize, this requires riding oneself of a victim-focused identity and the belief that one is disadvantaged and incapable of excellence. It requires the realization by people entering and advancing in the job market that nobody else is responsible for them as individuals. Herman Cain, black CEO of Godfather's Pizza chain, says that, "If you want to get anything out of this life, you better look at the situation the way it is in order to figure out how you overcome it. Who said life was supposed to be fair?"[37]

- A longer-term need is to broaden the base of the black middle class. One option is to encourage African Americans to engage in a wider range of occupations, such as engineering, information systems, and the professions, which produce higher incomes. Another is to increase black entrepreneurship and business ownership, a matter which will be discussed in more detail in Chapter Six. Note that all meaningful options depend directly on a high level of education.

6

Business — An Essential Institution in Empowerment

Black-owned businesses don't want charity. We have never asked for it. We don't want corporate handouts. We don't want to be treated as second-class business. And above all, we don't want to be treated as if doing business with us fulfills some sort of good will.

EARL GRAVES

Wherever you spend your money is where you create a job. If you live in Harlem and spend your money in Chicago, you create jobs for people in Chicago. If you are black and the businesses are run by people who are not black, then these people come in at 9:00 a.m., leave at 5:00 p.m., and take the wealth to the communities in which they live.

W. E. B. DU BOIS

THE primary route to economic security and self-sufficiency in the United States has always been through the ownership of business, and business is an institution of critical importance to the black community as it seeks empowerment.

Sol Ahiarah points out that blacks can solve most of their problems by owning and controlling their means of livelihood. Statistics show that ethnic groups with the highest business ownership rates have the highest mean incomes, while those with the lowest business ownership rates have the lowest mean income levels.[1]

Three decades ago African Americans, by dint of great courage, hard work, and a steely sense of purpose and commitment, won back the political and civil rights that had been taken from them. But securing legal rights was not the end of the struggle. Instead, it meant that black Americans would be able to shift more of their energy, thought, and resources from legal rights to securing economic justice. Martin Luther King Jr., Whitney M. Young, Jr., and Malcolm X were among those who understood that gaining and wisely using economic power was the next civil rights frontier. As J. I. Smith recently wrote in *The Buffalo News,* "Civil rights without economic strength is a borrowed event. It can be taken away at any time."[2]

The most promising path to economic power for black Americans today is through business. Business opportunities have abounded for decades, but blacks have failed to use their enormous purchasing power to their own benefit. A substantially greater number of black Americans must become entrepreneurs and own businesses.

"If we own businesses, we have the ability to hire people in our community and hopefully they'll spend in the community and allow the money to circulate even more," columnist William Raspberry said recently. "Our tendency is to turn the money over once and it's gone. The more business you do with black businesses, the more opportunity that your brother has to bring his business up to where you think it ought to be."[2]

This focus for black Americans is not new. The extraordinary development of black businesses from the end of the Civil War through the 1920s proved that blacks possessed a strong entrepreneurial spirit and could carve their own place in a freewheeling market economy. That spirit was among the things the Supreme Court's *Plessy* decision of 1896 was meant to destroy, and it was dimmed by the legal denial of rights through the segregation constitutions of many Southern states at the start of the 21st century.

That spirit must be rekindled. Through the remarkable phenomenon called globalization, the world is on the march economically, and those who do not march in step with it are likely to be run over and left in the dust. All around the globe, there is a deep commitment to capitalism and to the market economy. This a world that we have to prepare ourselves and our children to navigate. African Americans must develop an acute sense of economic awareness and entrepreneurial energy.

The revitalization of economic enterprise among African Americans needs to be married to the goal of improving educational opportunity for and the academic performance of African American youth. Black youth must have the skills and the inspiration necessary to compete at a world-class level if African Americans as a group are to build up their economic strength and security.

General education in business operation is also important. The Urban League has always focused on education. In 1993, the Los Angeles branch opened a business development and training center to teach black would-be entrepreneurs the fine points of starting and managing their own businesses. The center also provides technical assistance and information to people operating small businesses.[4]

Among the many needs to be addressed are economic literacy, including such things as obtaining credit, shopping for favorable interest rates, building equity, and using banks. Also needed are the basic skills of business management.

I. The Status of Black Business Ownership

The number of black-owned businesses in the United States has increased progressively since 1972. In the 1987 to 1992 period, the increase was 46 percent, from 424,165 businesses to 620,912. During this period, receipts for these firms increased 63 percent, from $19.8 billion to $32.2 billion. In comparison, the total number of firms in the country increased 26 percent in the 1987 to 1992, and overall receipts increased 67 percent, from $2 trillion to $3 trillion.

Two-thirds of African American businesses in 1992 were in the service or retail trades, and receipts per firm averaged $52,000. This compares with $193,000 per firm for the total U.S. Approximately 94 percent of African American firms in 1992 were sole proprietorships, that is, unincorporated businesses owned by individuals. Partnerships, which are unincorporated business owned by two or more persons, and small corporations comprised 2 and 4 percent respectively.[5]

While these trends are promising, overall figures show that blacks are still far from owning their proportionate share of American businesses.

African Americans constitute over 12 percent of the national population, but they own fewer than two percent of all businesses. This is in spite of controlling more than $350 billion in spending power.[6]

According to *Black Economics,* there are 108 business starts for every 1,000 Arabs in America. For Asians, there are 96 starts per 1,000, and there are 64 starts for whites. By contrast, there are only nine business starts for every 1,000 African Americans.[7]

To summarize, the news on black businesses is both good and bad. Black business ownership has increased at a slow, steady pace in the past 30 years, but the rate of increase has been far too small to meet the larger needs of the community.

II. Factors Which Determine Business Success

A large majority of new businesses which are started in the United States fail within five years, and the failure rate of business start-ups by blacks is 85 percent.[8] Once a business gets through its initial most-difficult growth period, chances of success improve considerably.

Generally, two broad sets of factors determine whether a business succeeds. First are those which are external and beyond the owners' direct control. The other set is internal to the business itself and to the people who run it and work in it. Internal factors are directly controllable by the owner.

Among the external factors which are essential to business, Ahiarah has identified: (1) access to capital, (2) availability of a relevant labor force, (3) access to supplies and raw materials, (5) ability to obtain customers and new markets, (5) access to supporting services, (6) availability of required facilities, and (7) a receptive population.[9] The climate in the United States, unfortunately, has never been very favorable to black-owned businesses.

Competition is another important external factor. To succeed, a business must be able to face competition, and this requires that it be good at what it does. The trend toward a global economy is increasing the number of competitors American firms have to face. Quality and customer satisfaction are more important than ever.

There are also a number of internal factors which interact to determine whether a business is successful. First and foremost, of course, are the competence, knowledge, dedication, and determination of the person or persons who are the organizers. The experience of personnel, their willingness from the top down to work hard, and their possession of and ability to utilize relevant technical know-how are crucial.

Second is the viability of the venture idea. Often this can only be determined through preliminary research and study. Third is planning, a key step often overlooked. Fourth is the right contacts. Business involves a great deal of networking among relevant people, and personal contacts can be decisive.

One of the largest causes of business failure is poor management. Year after year the lack of managerial experience and aptitude has accounted for around 90 percent of all failures analyzed by Dun & Bradstreet, Inc.

Successful businesses have entrepreneurs who know their business inside-out. They immerse themselves in the day-to-day operations with an eye toward future growth and toward paying bills at the end of each month. Entrepreneurs who fail usually don't understand that good intentions are not the same as experience.

III. Starting a Business

Hopefully, many people who read this book will think seriously of going into their own business. Running a business of your own will bring a sense of independence and an opportunity to use your own ideas. You will be boss and can't be fired. You will have a chance for higher income because you can collect a salary plus a profit or return on your investment. You will experience a pride in ownership. You can achieve the great satisfaction of building a valuable product for which there is a market. By being boss you can adopt new ideas quickly, and this flexibility will be one of your greatest assets.

These are some of the advantages and pleasures of operating your own business. But let us take a look at the other side.

If you have employees, you must meet a payroll week after week, and this includes salary, social security payments, and income taxes. You must always have money to pay the people who sell you goods and materials, the dealer who furnishes you fixtures and equipment, the mortgage holder or the landlord if you rent, the publisher running your advertisements, the tax collector, and many others. You must accept sole responsibility for all final decisions. Wrong judgment on your part can result in losses not only to yourself but to your employees, creditors, and customers as well. Moreover, you must withstand adverse situations caused by circumstances beyond your control, such as depressed economic conditions or strong competition.

No matter what business you choose, whether manufacturing, wholesaling, retailing, or service, you must satisfy your customer. Health authorities and insurance people will see that you meet certain standards and follow certain regulations. You will have to abide by wage and hour laws and keep records according to requirements of the tax system.

In deciding whether or not to start the venture, the first question you should ask is, "Am I the type to operate a business?" In answering, you should honestly appraise your strong points and weak points.

One study of small business managers showed that successful managers were distinguished by these personality characteristics: drive, thinking ability, human relations ability, communications ability, and technical knowledge. Do you have these in sufficient quantity?

Following are nine questions which will help you evaluate whether you are the type to run your own business. Add others that you think are significant for the type of business you desire to establish. Then rate yourself. You will do even better by asking a friend to have you rated anonymously by several people who know you. These should be people who can and will evaluate you objectively. The results may startle you. Be honest. Remember, in starting your own business, you are risking your money and your time.

1. Are you a self-starter?
2. Do you like and get along with other people?

3. Can you lead others?
4. Can you take responsibility?
5. Are you a good organizer?
6. Can you make tough decisions?
7. Can people trust what you say?
8. Can you stick with it?
9. Is your health good?

Can you honestly answer "yes" to most of these questions? You will do well to recognize your weak points before opening your business. Perhaps you can compensate for them by hiring the right help or obtaining associates whose strong points offset your weak ones. If you are weak in too many of the traits needed for managing a business, do not undertake the venture.

In the final analysis, it is up to you. Will your management be competent? Will you be able to judge and satisfy your customers' wants? Can you do this well enough that risks due to factors beyond your control will be compensated for?

Next you should decide what business you should choose. You might begin by writing a summary of your background and experience. Include experience in jobs, in school, and in your hobbies. Write down what you would like to do. Try to match up what you would like to do with your past experience. If you do not like the business you choose, your lack of enthusiasm may lead to failure. Remember that the more experience and training you have had which can be put to direct use in operating a particular enterprise, the better your chances of success.

Education will help, too. In almost all businesses, you must know how to figure interest and discounts, keep simple and adequate records, and conduct necessary correspondence. Many businesses today require technical knowledge that can only be obtained through education.

The new economy has created many new business opportunities. Many functions which were once performed in-house by large, self-sufficient manufacturers are being farmed out to small firms, a practice called out-sourcing. Innovative small firms with the technology and expertise to compete enjoy the advantages of flexibility and are often more proficient in gaining access to key information.

Some "hot" business opportunities identified in a recent study include:

- *Direct Sales.* From 1991 to 1995, the Direct Selling Association charted a 38 percent growth in direct retail sales, and an increase of 41 percent in the number of people involved in the industry.
- *Internet Advertising.* With more than 42 million adult Americans currently online, the Internet is gradually positioning itself as a powerful advertising medium — and a great place to start up a business.
- *Child Transport.* The child transport industry is gaining momentum as never before. The National Child Transport Association reported that membership increased threefold in 1996 alone.
- *Travel Assistance.* Travel expenditures are increasing in the African American community as disposable income increases. African American Historical Tours of Philadelphia offers tours of historic black landmarks in Philadelphia, Baltimore, Washington, and New York.
- *Computer Consultation in Homes.* The number of home computers in the country is growing rapidly, and they need servicing. Consultants who make house calls for computers are especially hot.
- *Herb Growing and Marketing.* As the general public becomes more and more interested in alternate health remedies, a larger number of people are taking natural supplements, most of them plant-based. Supplying these is a growing business opportunity.
- *Medical Transcription.* In an effort to cut expenses, many hospitals have begun to outsource their transcription responsibilities, and this makes the medical-transcription businesses an excellent opportunity.
- *Meal Delivery.* Diners across the country are having their favorite restaurant dishes delivered to them, and a growing number of restaurants use outside delivery services. According to a recent study, about one out of ten of these had meals delivered by an outside service in 1995, compared with practically none in 1992.[10]

After selecting the type of business, the next step — and this is a crucial one — is to prepare a strategic plan. This is a difficult, time-consuming task, but remember that the number one reason businesses fail is the lack of adequate planning prior to startup.

Management Quarterly identifies these sections as needed in a business plan:

- Executive Summary, which includes a clear statement of purpose, a feasibility study, and a needs assessment.
- Market Analysis and Marketing Strategy.
- Management, including key managers and directors, organizational structure, plans for future staff, and expected compensation.
- Operations Plans, with space and equipment requirements, working capital requirements, and lending and investment criteria.
- Financial Statements and Projections, including three-years of pro forma financial statements which include income, cash flow, balance sheets, and break-even analysis.
- Funding Sources, with expected amounts and capitalization.
- Summary of Risks Involved, including assumptions associated with each section of the business plan and contingency plans for potential problems and delays.[11]

Estimating the amount needed requires careful study and investigation. Remember that one of the principal causes of failure among businesses is inadequate financing. Money needs will vary according to the type of operation (manufacturing, wholesaling, retailing, or servicing), the kind of merchandise or services handled, income level of your business, general economic conditions at the time of starting, and many other factors.

First, estimate your sales volume. This will depend on the total amount of business in the area, the number and ability of direct competitors, and your own capability to compete for the consumer's dollar. You may obtain assistance in making your sales estimate from wholesalers, trade associations, your banker, and other businessmen. Include the amount of profit you hope the business will produce.

In reaching your final estimate of sales do not be over-optimistic. A new business generally grows slowly. If you overestimate sales you are likely to invest too much in equipment and initial inventory and to commit yourself to heavier operating expenses than your actual sales volume will justify.

Costs for startup and recurring inventory must be considered. In estimating inventory for a wholesaling or retailing business, suggestions may be sought from prospective suppliers of merchandise.

In addition to continuing monthly expenses you must add costs which occur only once. Advice on layout and selection of fixtures and equipment can be obtained from representatives of equipment manufacturers and trade associations.

Your available money should exceed by a safe margin the estimated cash you need to start. This is because you not only need money to get started, but enough in reserve to carry the business until it becomes self-supporting. The time required varies from a few months to four or five years.

If you do not have sufficient cash, remember you may be unable to:

1. Afford enough employees to keep the business operating.
2. Invest in proper equipment.
3. Maintain an adequate stock of merchandise or materials to build sales volume.
4. Take advantage of discounts offered by creditors and thereby avoid heavy interest penalties.
5. Grant customers credit to meet competition.

After you have chosen the type of business you will start and completed your plan, you are ready to select a location. While it is important to choose a spot in which you will be happy, you should make sure the community needs the business you have decided to open. Picking the exact location involves the selection of the town or city, then the area within the town or city, and finally a specific site. You need to investigate zoning laws before making the final decision of where to locate. The best place to learn about local zoning laws is usually the city hall.

At this point, you are ready to secure needed financing. The amount you need can come from you, personal friends, or family, but it will be very difficult for someone to invest in you if you have not invested in yourself. In most cases, it is necessary to finance through a bank or other financial institution. Before obtaining too large a share of the money from outside sources, remember that you should retain sufficient personal control to assure yourself ownership.

The main outside sources of money in the early days of your business will probably be the commercial bank and the trade creditor or equipment manufacturer. Other possibilities include small loan companies, factoring companies, commercial credit companies, sales finance companies, and insurance companies.

You should become well acquainted with your banker. In selecting a banker, consider his progressiveness, his attitude toward business, the credit services he offers, and the size and management policies of his bank. Does the banker have an interested, helpful attitude toward your problems? Will the bank consider a term loan or accept receivables as security for a loan? Does it have other services, such as a foreign exchange department and facilities for handling installment transactions? How deeply is the bank concerned with the growth and prosperity of your local community?

If you can show that you have carefully worked out your financial requirements, have a good business plan, and can demonstrate experience and integrity, you have a good chance of financing through a lending institution.

When you deal with your banker, sell yourself. Openly discuss your plans and difficulties with him. It is his business not to betray confidence. Remember that before a banker is prepared to make a loan he must feel satisfied with answers to these questions:

1. What sort of person are you?
2. What are you going to do with the money?
3. When and how do you plan to pay it back?
4. Does the amount make suitable allowance for unexpected developments?
5. What is the outlook for you, for your line of business, and for business in general?

One key way to go into business is through the joint venture, in which you share ownership with one or more other persons. This approach is especially useful if you cannot get the capital you need or if you lack expertise. A joint venture can work quite well as long as other parties to it have adequate financing and the operational know-how of the enterprise. Needless to say, great care must be taken in selecting other parties to the venture. Personality and character, as well as ability to render technical or financial assistance, affect the success of a partnership.

If you have associates, should your legal organization be a partnership or a corporation? In a partnership, as in a single proprietorship, the owners are personally responsible for the debts of the firm, even if it exceeds the amount they have invested. In a corporation, the liability of the owners is limited to the amount they pay for their shares of stock. Even with no partners you may decide a corporation with minor stockholders is better than a single proprietorship, primarily because of the limited liability of a corporation.

Some of the other common start-up essentials are:

1. Obtain a federal Employer Identification Number (EIN). The EIN allows the federal government to keep track of tax amounts withheld for employees and any funds paid to independent contractors. To get one, file IRS Form SS-4.
2. Apply for state and city business licenses. Contact the business license bureau in your city or county to find out what kind of business license, if any, you need to purchase. Also, check with any local or

state agencies that may have jurisdiction over occupational licenses related to your type of business.

3. Obtain state sales tax and resale tax certificates. If you plan to sell goods directly to the public, you'll need a state sales tax certificate so that you can submit sales tax payments to the state. If you will be buying raw materials wholesale from distributors or selling goods wholesale to shops and other distributors, you'll need a resale tax certificate so that no sales taxes will be collected for such transactions.

5. Register your business name. If you will conduct your business using a business name that does not contain your full legal name as part of it, you will need to file a DBA ("doing business as"), also commonly known as a fictitious name statement. DBAs are generally filed at the county clerk's office.[12]

IV. The Power and Relevance of Business Incubators

Della Clark, president of the Philadelphia Enterprise Center, says that the greatest ills plaguing minority businesses are the lack of a cash reserve, the lack of collateralized assets, and the lack of real business experience. Clark's Center is a business incubator for minority clients. She joins many others in the conviction that business incubators can significantly assist black entrepreneurial efforts.[13]

Business incubators are designed to help minimize the early hurdles in starting a small business and come in many sizes and specialties. Incubators provide low-cost space and give entrepreneurs access to equipment and services they might be unable to afford otherwise. Their combination of below-market rents, shared business services, and management assistance has helped a large number of new businesses start successfully.[14]

Among services incubators typically provide are business plan review and preparation, technical advice on product design and production, marketing and sales support, legal advice, referrals for financial resources, and assistance in securing contracts. Many offer training programs to help their clients become creditworthy. They have access to a talent bank of professionals such as accountants, lawyers, sales representatives, and management consultants.[15]

To become a client of an incubator, a person must have thought through his or her proposed business carefully. Typically, the business incubator has a board of directors which reviews the applications of and interviews prospective clients. If the board determines that the business has a chance to succeed, it is accepted. Most incubator clients stay two to four years.[16]

About 14 percent of incubators are affiliated with universities and colleges. Forty-four percent are subsidized by the government, primarily through the Small Business Administration, and by nonprofit organizations. About 14 percent are financed by private firms, and 19 percent are funded by a combination of private and public financing.[17]

There are now about 530 business incubators in the U.S. and Canada, and 30 are targeted at minority businesses. The success rate of incubators which serve minority clients compares favorably with that of other incubators. A recent study revealed that, of the 4,000 plus firms started in incubators, 80 percent are still in operation after several years. This compares to an 80 percent failure rate for other new businesses.[18]

Most incubators cater to manufacturing, service, or high-tech companies and are not likely to accept retail businesses, mainly because their limited success with retail operations. There is no reason that retail business cannot be assisted, however, if the incubator is specifically designed to provide the assistance needed.

We believe that, without question, business incubators are a powerful tool to help black entrepreneurs get established successfully. This concept deserves a great deal more attention than it is currently receiving, and a significant number of new incubators for minorities should be started.

These steps should be followed in planning a business incubator:

1. Analyze the local small business base and determine the potential for growth in the community. Assess the potential sources of support such as accountants, lawyers, university small business development

centers, and private sector business groups.

2. Identify a target group and develop a marketing plan. Using the data from step one, determine the most realistic business and the way clients will be recruited and selected.

3. Identify a suitable site and determine the cost for initial renovation. If possible, pick a site with suitable truck docks, a railroad spur, and highway access. Using services of the city or county, cost out the necessary renovations.

4. Evaluate the availability of public sector and private funds. A wide range of state and federal programs have helped incubators.

5. Provide for central business services. The incubator should provide a range of services, as discussed above. One solution is to locate the incubator in a private firm that can provide most of the needed services.

6. Develop a management plan. A successful incubator needs close, detailed management. The plan should include businesses to be supported, services to be offered, and client selection.

V. Unity and Support Networks

African Americans starting businesses need special dedication and very often special help. Ahiarah's comment that there has never been a level playing field is true, and his prediction that there will probably not be one in the near future is probably valid.[18] In most cases, therefore, the special help for new businesses must come from within the black community.

Financing, developing markets, and establishing interpersonal relationships have been identified as special needs. The black community has the resources to meet these needs if it can muster sufficient unity and develop a comprehensive support network. Favorable government policies will help and should be pursued, but these cannot be counted on.

Securing the capital needed to start a business and take it to viability no longer has to be a problem because Black America now controls significant financial resources. The problem is organizing them and making them available. The personal income of Black Americans after taxes was estimated at $399 billion in 1995. This was up 33.9 percent from 1990. This increase is more than the 29.5 percent growth rate estimated for the total U.S. in the same period and more than twice the inflation rate. The income level is projected to exceed $550 billion by the turn of the century.[20]

Why should there be a problem in gaining access to capital when this gigantic sum is controlled by the black community? Black activists place much of the blame on black people themselves. "We talk Black and spend White," says Pearl Murphy, cofounder of the African-American Business Association in Washington, D.C.[21]

Sol Ahiarah is among those who make the point that racial solidarity is needed in addressing the problem of financing. The framework for black capitalism, he says, should have a group emphasis rather than the individualistic emphasis now followed. By ignoring the importance of a communal approach in shaping minority economic development, many effective ways to accomplish revitalization are overlooked.[22]

Karen R. Gunn, executive director of the Urban Merchants Assistance Corporation in Chicago, comments, "It's unfortunate that we exercise our options outside our community," and she says there would be many more options "if we stood behind each other."[23] Jawannza Kunjufu, author of *Black Economics: Solutions for Economic and Community Empowerment*, observes that "We only spend seven percent of our $360 billion with each other."[24] In a similar vein, Henry C. Alford, Chairman and CEO of the National Black Chamber of Commerce in Washington, D.C., blames "our naivete" and ignorance in failing to recognize the importance of trading with each other and the importance of recycling the dollar within the black community. "We as a people don't see the need of investing in our own community."[25]

The National Black Business Trade Association, Inc. stated in a recent press release, "We must do business with ourselves. We must spend money with ourselves. We must demand excellence in service from ourselves! We must teach our youth about business and the opportunities available to them for the future."[26]

A requirement for success in today's business environment is access to knowledge and information. This is accomplished in part through social groups and professional networks, that is, through knowing and associating with the right people.

Gaining needed information has been a problem for black businessmen because they are often excluded from the networking system in place. Dawn Clements observed in a recent *Minority Business Entrepreneur* article that very few professional networks exist for minority-owned firms in the financial services industry. She advocates determined development of such networks. "You and your business will profit," she says, in increased knowledge and political clout.[27]

Among national organizations working to help with this need are The National Black Business Trade Association (NBBTA), which has designed a program to teach African Americans how to do business, and the National Black Chamber of Commerce. Several universities are involved in promoting black business. Far too little is done, however, at the local level, partly because networking does not extend there.

As we noted in Chapter Two, the most logical organization to meet the diverse needs of organizing financial support, promoting business, and developing local self-help support networks is the black church. Black churches can and must play a central role in achieving needed unity and in providing support. The church can also play a lead role in establishing business incubators.

Deborah Evans, a theological student whose studies are focused on the Black Church and Economic Development, outlines in more detail the role the church must play. Evans is a graduate of California State University at Hayward, she holds an MBA from Harvard, and is working on her Masters of Theological Studies at Harvard Divinity School.

"Now that we are facing this global economy," Evans says, "the church has been unable to help the black community push through or confront these issues effectively. We must educate our black clergy around economics, how to amass wealth, how to understand wealth, how to create jobs, and how to understand capital and credit. . . . We cannot move forward in talking about economic and business development without dealing with the black church. The church must be the cornerstone of development in the black community."[28]

THERE is no acceptable reason why a people the size of the African American community, with its collective income, is not a major force in the mainstream of the American economy and why the number of black-owned businesses is not much larger. Successful business ownership and the economic power that goes with it is the ultimate guarantee of independence and self-sufficiency in the United States.

While noting the legacy of slavery and the reality of a racism that manifests itself in the denial of bank loans and second-rate schools, black activists place much of the blame for the poor state of black business on black people. They say that blacks often deny other blacks support in business and that blacks with corporate jobs sell their talents and spend their dollars outside their communities.

Blacks must husband their individual and collective resources and invest them wisely to acquire the wealth, the net financial assets, needed to lessen their dependence on income through the weekly paycheck. In doing this, they can more powerfully direct their resources to support black institutions from local churches and community organizations to historically black colleges and universities.

Black Americans must increase their ownership of businesses, small, medium, and large. They must build up local business districts in black neighborhoods, in the suburbs as well as the inner cities, so that they can provide jobs for residents of those areas and truly possess the land on which they live. They must increase the number of African Americans holding significant positions in the revenue-producing divisions of corporate America.

This is the way it has worked for other Americans. Each group contributed to the growth of the American economy, and working through the political process, took for itself a share of the resources. So it must be for African Americans and other people of color.

To prepare themselves and their children to navigate the new, more economically challenging environment of globalization, African American must embrace and pass along the acute sense of economic awareness and entrepreneurial energy that produced an extraordinary growth of black-owned businesses in America from the end of the Civil War to the 1920s. Despite the barriers which still exist, blacks must make that zest for economic achievement soar.

African Americans are still on the frontier, and their journey to a place of security and safety is just as challenging today as it was in earlier decades of this century. As we approach the beginning of the 21st century, even as we take stock of and appreciate the significant progress made since the 1960s, efforts to gain economic strength must be intensified.

Total Involvement in the National Agenda

Black people keep forgetting that they are black — it's amazing that we do, because no one else does. For years blacks have searched hard and long to find someone or some group of people that they can fault for their inadequacies. It would be wise at this point, if they would look in the mirror.

JESSE J. LEWIS

This the American black man knows: his fight is a fight to the finish. Either he dies or he wins. He will enter modern civilization in America as a black man on terms of perfect and unlimited equality with any white man, or he will enter not at all. Either extermination root and branch or absolute equality. There can be no compromise. This is the last great battle of the west.

W. E. B. DU BOIS

THE world fast approaches a new century and a new millennium. It is a time for new beginnings and new hope, a time to put aside the failures and disappointments of the past and to resolve to build a better future. Black America has the greatest opportunity in its history to achieve full empowerment — to experience the dignity of full citizenship and to move into the mainstream of American life, aware of its history and accomplishments, proud of its identity, and confident of the future.

At the same time there is danger that the opportunity will not be seized and that a full third of black America, over 11 million souls who live in the inner city, will sink further into despair and hopelessness. Inner-city residents are faced every day with gangs, violence, theft, broken families, teenage pregnancy, poverty, terrible living conditions

for the elderly, and poor schooling. Solving their problems requires a
level of effort seldom mounted by the United States in addressing
domestic issues.

Vernon Jordan recently commented that there are two possible paths
for Americans as we enter the next century. First is the path of progress
toward building multiracial societies and more harmonious interracial
discourse. The second, however, is continued polarization, a path marked
by black-white frictions and growing racial disadvantage in the United
States and the world. The path we choose, Jordan says, will determine
whether the 21st century is one of peace and prosperity for all of the
world's peoples or a century of racial strife and misery.[1]

Manning Marable writes that, "Those blacks who are on the path of
upward mobility in terms of education, job opportunities, and financial
income will do twice as good in the next four years in as in the last eight
years." But, he predicts, "During the years to come, blacks and other
minorities who are less fortunate than the average American, will have
the most difficult times of their lives." Many things have improved, but
on a range of substantive issues affecting the lives of millions of working
class and impoverished African Americans, little has changed.[2]

I. The Case for Hope

In considering the case for hope, we examine first the unique history
of African Americans. When other immigrant groups came to this
country, they had a continuous, predictable experience that led from
great struggles by the first arrivals to find jobs and survive to movement
into mainstream America in a generation or two. They had a clear image
of their past and an understanding of the cultural heritage they brought
with them.

This is not true for black Americans. "The history of African Americans in the United States from 1619 to the present provides a classic
example of cultural and psychological discontinuity in the development
of a people," observes president Clarence Hughes, of Bowie State
University.[3]

Black Americas have lived through five distinct periods. First were the years from 1509 to 1670 when most blacks came to this country by their own choice and not as slaves. Next was the period of slavery, from about 1670 to 1865. Third was Reconstruction and the new South era, which lasted from 1865 to 1905 and saw the nation back away from its promise of full citizenship. Fourth was the Jim Crow era, from 1905 to 1955, in which blacks were legally denied the rights of citizenship. And finally is the current period which began with the Civil Rights Movement in 1955.[4]

The black experience in America inevitably resulted in a deep sense of uncertainty and rootlessness and a break in the thread of cultural identity. Being called inferior and treated so by the larger society and being denied basic human rights for most of some 290 years raised inescapable questions of self-worth and self-esteem.

While the civil rights revolution was a victory in the fight for equality and freedom, its aftermath required major readjustment, with social disorganization and a new, necessary effort at self-identification. Dr. Edward W. Robinson, Jr., a retired insurance company president from Philadelphia, has devoted his life to giving African Americans a pride in their African heritage. "I am fighting two kinds of prejudice," he says. "First is the self-hatred that leads to poor self-esteem and has tragic consequences for blacks and second is the contempt of American society in general for people of African descent."[5]

Fortunately, the historic discontinuities have ended, and the path ahead will not involve the disastrous redefinitions and changes in status of the past. As gains were consolidated after 1965, black Americans made remarkable progress in a number of areas. These changes have not occurred as fast as many people would have liked, but most social change is gradual. In fact, the progress of black America in the last 30 years has, from the perspective of history, been unprecedented in scope and speed.

There is reason to believe that the country has achieved a "critical mass" in the move toward equality and that there is no turning back. Blacks are understood by all segments of society, including the most loathsome hate-mongers, to be full citizens with all the rights thereto. In a larger sense, the country is redefining itself as a diverse society rather than a white Anglo-Saxon society with little side pockets of "others."

Can we now expect the racism and bigotry that has tarnished America to disappear? The answer, obviously, is "no." Boston College professor Elaine Inderhughes defines racism as an element of "social structure," and adds that in America it is largely a belief in the superiority of whites and the inferiority of people-of-color.[6] Such attitudes are deeply ingrained and will continue to be a problem.

Racism will not disappear, but it will continue to diminish. There is strong evidence that attitudes follow behavior,[7] and it is clear that the racial attitudes of a significant number of Americans changed positively in the last three decades. As blacks and whites more frequently encounter each other face-to-face on an equal-status basis, in everyday life, in the media and in the courts, attitudes will continue to evolve.

OTHER positive trends add to feelings of hope. A recent government report provided evidence that, after decades of struggling, the nation's cities are beginning to rebound. However, there are still great problems. The inner cities remain intensely isolated communities in which joblessness is high, poverty is rampant, drug addiction is flourishing, and genuine opportunities are hard to come by. But crime is decreasing, municipal budgets are in much better shape, and there are unmistakable signs of renewal, even in hard-core areas

Robert Herbert of *The New York Times* tells of men and women across the country who have rolled up their sleeves and built new housing. "In the really tough neighborhoods, they are the unheralded heroes," he says. "Working with churches and small community organizations, they pulled off surprising early successes. New homes would go up on a block, or old buildings would be renovated, and before long a startling transformation would occur. New families are drawn to the neighborhood and a new sense of pride can be seen. Graffiti and other forms of vandalism tend to occur less frequently."[8] Earlier in this book is the story of the BEAT organization's success in the inner city of Birmingham, Alabama.

Another item of good news is that, after a steady drop through the 1990s, the birth rate for unmarried black women reached a record low in 1996. As with other problems, much more improvement is required. A much larger percent of single black women than single white women had a child out of wedlock. Still, the birth rate for single black women was the lowest level since the government began recording the statistic in 1969.[9]

A third significant item is the accelerating growth of the economic power of black America. Recent Census Bureau figures show that, during the last five years of economic prosperity, the household incomes of black Americans have increased 16.8 percent, three times faster than the nation as a whole. This is a remarkable rate of growth, and it has pushed poverty among blacks to a record low, with 1.7 million going off the poverty rolls. Unemployment among blacks has dropped below 10 percent, the lowest in 25 years.

The average household income for black Americans grew to $25,050, and this translates into big gains in buying power and opportunities for new businesses. A study by the Selig Center for Economic Growth at the University of Georgia projects that black buying power in the United States will increase from the $308 billion of 1990 to $533 billion in 1999. This is a remarkable story which supports our contention that blacks have sufficient economic strength to reach full empowerment. The down side, which shows that the fight is far from over, is that average white income is $38,970, almost $14,000 more than blacks.[10]

IN THE last 30 years, Republicans have turned race into a "wedge" issue in the attempt to separate working- and middle-class whites from the Democratic party. Beginning with the election of Ronald Reagan and continuing through the Presidency of George Bush, this strategy, which we call the Reagan/Bush white counter-revolution, has resulted in a backlash against equal rights. The backlash was most pronounced among working-class, middle-income whites who found themselves threatened by the growing opportunities for blacks and by such initiatives as affirmative action and quotas.[11]

The Clinton Presidency may mark the end of the counter-revolution.

The President's appointments to his cabinet and to the federal judiciary give evidence of his own commitment, and he made strong pleas in his 1996 campaign and in his second inaugural address for the country to solve the remaining problems related to racial differences. Recently he has conducted a series of meetings in different locations designed to confront racial problems honestly and discuss possible solutions.

There is no doubt that when the American people spoke in 1996, they said President Clinton did an excellent job during his first term and deserved another four years. His enemies, however, intensified an attempt begun when he was still governor of Arkansas to weaken and destroy him. A wide-ranging investigation, which began with alleged misconduct in a land development project, finally focused on accusations of sexual misconduct with White House intern Monica Lewinsky and lying in public. This led to an impeachment investigation in the House of Representatives, where Republicans held a majority of seats.

Republican losses in the 1998 election were a clear signal that the American people did not consider the Lewinsky matter a sufficient reason to remove Clinton from office. The people indicated, rather, that they wanted their elected officials in Washington to cut out the bickering and get to work on the country's business.

The 1988 election results showed again that the great majority of Americans wish to have their elected officials in the middle of the political spectrum. Republicans who won tended to be in the mold of George W. and Jeb Bush, whose general outlook was called compassionate conservatism. The mean-spirited, rigid self-righteousness of the far right and the Christian Coalition took a beating. The drift to the right in the United States appeared to have ended. In larger perspective, the 1998 elections suggested that the people want to continue progress toward a better, more fair society. The elections also showed the power of black participation in the political process.

II. Separatism, Unity, and the Mainstream

Since pre-Civil War days African Americans have debated the question of whether it is in their best interest to be amalgamated into the larger society or to be separated from it. Historical discontinuity and the discrimination and humiliation perpetrated by white America has infused this question with strong passions and honest differences. Clarence Hughes identifies three current approaches to this matter as Africentrism, self-help, and traditional civil rights.

Africentrism is similar to the separatist positions of the past and calls for the separation of blacks in America from the larger society. The self-help view stresses economic development and self-sufficiency of blacks within the mainstream culture and holds that Africentrism is self-defeating. The traditional civil rights view holds that the larger society is responsible for centuries of depravation, and it demands compensation and help in overcoming the effects, while seeking assimilation.[12]

In reviewing these options, we must remember that the question is not the failures of the past but prospects for the future. The only realistic path to empowerment is Hughes's self-help option within a broadened American mainstream. As Professor Michelle Wallace of the City College of New York writes, "(black) nationalism is not going to have a part in the 21st century unless things go terribly poorly. Its time has passed."[13]

As noted earlier, an African-American Leadership Summit hosted by the NAACP in Baltimore in June 1994 supported the middle position of movement to the mainstream at the same time there is self-determination. The conference emphasized the necessity of coalition politics.

Louis Lomax wrote in *The Negro Revolt* that, "Whatever else the Negro is, he is American. Whatever he is to become — integrated, unintegrated, or disintegrated — he will become it in America. Our lot is irrevocably cast, and whatever future awaits America awaits the Negro. Whatever future awaits the Negro, awaits America."[15]

Moving to the mainstream does not imply that African Americans should give up their identity and mimic whites because the mainstream itself changes and broadens in time as the variety of people in the country increases. "Mainstream" represents the common core, the area of common values and interests that holds together the social fabric.

Through the first century and a half of American history, the country accepted the "melting pot" myth. It was a place where ethnic differences would be melted to produce a new homogeneous American, but an American in the European model. In the last fifty years, that notion has fallen by the wayside as the country has become more diverse. Rather than a melting pot, the more accurate metaphor for the population of the United States in 1998 is the "rainbow" which Jesse Jackson has suggested, a cultural pluralism in which blacks and others are aware of and guided by their cultural heritage.[16]

The population now is about 75 percent white. Census Bureau projections show that in fifty years it will be only 55 percent white. It will be 13 percent black, 22 percent Hispanic, and 11 percent Asian. As these changes occur, diversity is being recognized more and more as a source of great strength in America. The country, in proving that people of different races, religions, cultures, and views can work and live together, continues to broaden the concept of "mainstream." Black Americans can be in the mainstream and loyal to the country at the same time they are self-aware and stress black consciousness in politics, economics, and education.[17]

Black self-awareness refers to pride in one's historical roots, racial identity, and culture. It means determination to fight aggressively for full opportunity and commitment to use economic and political resources to support black businesses and institutions. It refers to holding the core values of black culture like freedom, justice, equality, and racial parity at all levels of human intercourse. In no way, however, do these imply separatism from American society as a whole.[18]

Self-help in the mainstream is the middle course between separatism and assimilation, and it is the only realistic option for black America now and in the future.

III. Essential Steps for Blacks and for the Larger Society

In a powerful article, Sol Ahiarah makes the point that, for empowerment to be fully achieved, there are essential steps for both blacks and for the larger society. Some of the change is cultural, Ahiarah notes, and is not just a matter of deciding to do things differently.[19] This, as we know, requires concerted effort over time and depends on institution building.

For blacks, the need is to solve the problems within. Dr. Shirley A. Thornton, executive director of the San Francisco Housing Authority, spoke eloquently to the need to solve problems within in her 1994 Charles H. Thompson Lecture-Colloquium Keynote Address.

"If we African Americans are to take responsibility for our own destiny," she said, "we have to stop shucking and jiving and half-stepping and accept the indisputable fact that, until we take responsibility for our own destiny, there will be no positive change in our condition."

"We must never forget that we are from a long line of survivors and that we have a responsibility to keep our families and communities intact, to work hard, to acquire knowledge, and, above all, to believe in ourselves." People who love themselves seek to preserve their lives and not destroy them, Thornton noted.[20]

To solve their own problems, blacks must grasp the power now at their disposal to secure equal treatment before the law and to participate in decisions which guide the economic life of the nation. They must be fully self-sufficient in bringing this about. They must grasp power because no one else will give it to them, and they must exercise it to protect their interests in the larger society. In the process, they must act on the realization that, outside of the spiritual realm, all power ultimately depends on economics.

Black people in this country cannot afford to be less than the best. They must dedicate themselves to doing everything better than anyone else. Their motto must be, "We are going to work harder, we are going to be more faithful, and we are going to be more honest." When blacks get in a position of trust, they must exercise responsibility so there can be no question of character and integrity. They must have better work ethics and more commitment to each other than any other race of people.

Blacks also have to be concerned with the image they project. Several suits have recently been won against major corporations in which blacks have been referred to as black jelly beans, lazy-bones, and niggers. It is difficult to make this point forcefully, however, when black stand-up comics make liberal use of the terms "black m-f" and "nigger."

THE REVITALIZATION of black institutions will not in itself assure that empowerment occurs because the larger society plays an essential, facilitating role. It is critical that America assure for the first time — absolutely and unquestionably — that the playing field is level. The country must do what it has failed in much of the past and assure that black citizens actually do enjoy all of the same rights as other citizens.

This means equal treatment before the law, in civil, criminal, and equity matters. It means full opportunity for every black American to develop and prosper according to individual abilities, energy, and motivation and not be constrained by artificial barriers. It means sharing with other citizens the freedom to act, speak, think, and otherwise enjoy life, limited only to the extent required to maintain an orderly society.

American ideals are based most fundamentally on the conviction that all humans are equal in the sight of God, and all deserve the same chance to succeed. It is imperative that the United States continue to make equality in the broadest sense a primary goal. The *laissez-faire* social Darwinism of the late-19th century, with its implicit assumption that those at the bottom deserve what they are getting, strayed far afield, and this kind of thinking threatens again in a time of prosperity and growing materialism. It is essential to our country's integrity that government at all levels continue the effort to improve opportunities for those deprived of a fair chance by accidental circumstances of birth. Affirmative action as we have know it is ending, and welfare is being redefined. These must be replaced with more effective ways to aid the disadvantaged.

We have no illusions that the larger society will make all of the needed changes without continued pressure. The pitfalls of racism and reaction, which have done such harm in the past, remain a temptation and are evident today in the rhetoric and motives of the far right. People of good will, of all races and backgrounds, must keep pushing hard to move the country to the facilitating position it should have.

Aside from moral and idealistic issues, there are very pragmatic reasons for society to make sure no person is held down artificially. In the comment quoted above, Louis Lomax makes the point that American society depends on the black future at the same time that the black future depends on American society. By facilitating black empowerment, America is assuring that all of its resources will be used and is protecting its future.

IN A MOVE that seems generally popular, the United States is reforming its welfare system. Most people apparently agree with Peter Drucker's assessment that welfare, as currently constructed, harms society and destroys people. Drucker says that in the United States, the welfare system effectively pays people for not working.[21]

A thoughtful, insightful article in the May 1, 1995, issue of *Money* magazine suggests, however, that we should proceed with great caution before making fundamental welfare changes. Otherwise, we are likely to do more harm than good.

To the extent that it harms poor people and makes them dependent, the social welfare system should be reformed. But in terms of decreasing the national budget, we must also carefully consider another type of welfare, "corporate welfare," which uses public funds to subsidize large corporations.

Social welfare is usually thought to consist of AFDC (Aid For Dependent Children), food and nutrition assistance, housing assistance, and Social Security payments to low-income aged, blind, and disabled. About half of the poor receive food stamps, 47 percent are covered by Medicaid, and 18 percent live in public housing.

These programs account for about 4.8 percent of the federal budget, or some $77 billion a year. This compares to $330 billion for Social Security, $292 billion for national defense, $165 billion for Medicare, and $203 billion in interest on the national debt, which increased from one trillion dollars to over three trillion under Presidents Reagan and Bush.[22]

According to Denise M. Topolnicki, the welfare reform package passed by Congress and signed by President Clinton is likely to increase the nation's poverty rate rather than decrease it. "Like previous well-intentioned prescriptions," Topolnicki asserts, "this new initiative rests on widely held but mistaken myths about the poor."[23]

For example:

- Myth: The Great Society's war on poverty made the problem worse. Fact: The poverty rate in 1964 was 19 percent. It is now 14.5 percent.
- Myth: Welfare dependence passes from one generation to the next. Fact: Two-thirds of kids whose parents collected welfare benefits between 1968 and 1988 did not receive them as adults.
- Myth: Poverty tends to be lifelong. Fact: Twenty percent of the poor people in a given year are not poor the following year. This is true even though about a third of the poor are elderly or disabled.
- Myth: Welfare costs are a major tax burden on the middle class. Fact: A family earning $50,000 annually contributes about $1.69 a day for programs that support welfare recipients.
- Myth: Work will take a person out of poverty. Fact: People on welfare find that jobs available to them usually earn too little to support a family. This is increasingly true as we move into the global economy.
- Myth: The poor have too many kids. Fact: The average poor family receiving AFDC has 2.9 members, compared with 3.2 for the population at large.
- Myth: Most of the poor live in inner-city ghettos. Fact: Only about one in eight poor Americans lives in the inner city.
- Myth: Most of the poor are black. Whites, with 83 percent of the total population, make up 67 percent of America's poor, while blacks, who comprise 13 percent of the total, make up 29 percent of the poor.

Three major assumptions about social welfare recipients are largely true:

- The poor are less educated than other Americans. Only 56 percent of poor household heads are high-school graduates, compared with 81 percent of all household heads.
- Most of the poor don't work. Only nine percent of poor working-age adults work full-time, year round, compared with 42 percent of all working-age adults.
- The poor tend to live in single-parent households headed by women. About 52 percent of poor families are headed by single females, compared with only 18 percent in the total population.[24]

Poor people have a difficult time escaping from poverty, whatever form social welfare takes. Statistics show that the best way out by far is through education, and it is incumbent on society to assure that, if they take this responsibility, the education they need is available.

In a bit of irony, what has been called "corporate welfare" has been estimated to cost the government anywhere from $60 billion to more than $100 billion annually. The term "corporate welfare" was coined by former Labor Secretary Robert Reich when he cited data from a Progressive Policy Institute report on wasteful federal subsidies to corporations. Reich referred to these subsidies as "aid to dependent corporations." Such items as agricultural subsidies, price supports, defense procurement, energy-related industry supports, and research and development are included. An estimated $35 billion yearly go to these activities. In addition are special tax provisions which cost the government approximately $20 billion a year.[25] Those receiving this kind of government aid are usually among the strongest opponents of government help to the poor.

THE INNER-CITY problem is a cancer on American Society. It affects directly the one-third of the black population which lives there, and it affects the larger society in the spillover of violence, lawlessness, and drugs. It is a direct challenge to American claims of fairness, equality, and opportunity.

The problems of the ghetto result from poverty, poor education, lack of jobs, absence of a support system, hopelessness, and the cultural confusion and disorganization which result. In short, essential institutions are missing. The poor, as usual, are the neglected victims, for they have no political power and no leverage.

The inner-city problem can be solved if society can muster the will. One sure way is through an urban Marshall Plan, as suggested by John Jacob, which directs the enormous resources of this nation to the task. The end of the Cold War resulted in an annual saving of about $150 billion in the national budget. Even if $100 billion or so were applied to deficit reduction, there would remain $50 billion which could be used to develop the economic infrastructure in the inner city and moved people out of poverty.[26]

Drug problems, thievery, murder, other crimes against the person, and a range of criminal behavior can be significantly reduced below current levels. As always, the best solution is to provide real opportunity and through education and jobs to give people an honest chance to better their own condition.

IV. Conclusion

Minorities in this country will have an opportunity to make more progress during the first decades of the 21st century than they have ever made before. However, they must first understand that this country is moving from manual power to technological power. It is moving from an industrial society to an information society.

Minorities must also understand that, regardless of the mergers of large corporations, the life blood of this country is still small business. In the last few years, minority business enterprise has increased significantly. This effort must be stepped up to a new level, and blacks must get involved in all types of business enterprise that is profitable.

Money is universally recognized as an influence. Why can't black people set as a goal for the immediate future to make a million millionaires? This may seem farfetched, but the process would be simple.

Suppose America's black athletes, black writers, and black actors would decide to employ black managers. For example, if Michael Jordan had a black manager and Tiger Woods had a black manager, these two individuals alone would put $2 million in the black community. What would happen if every black church in America went to a black savings and loan to deposit their revenues every Monday for 10 years?

During the past three or four decades, blacks have lost their neighborhood grocery stores, their neighborhood shoe shops, their neighborhood vegetable stands, their neighborhood restaurants, and their neighborhood service stations. They have lost everything but shade-tree mechanics, and these could be lost in the next two or three years because automobiles have become so complicated. Not many years ago, black people held all of the jobs at the major hotels and resorts. These days, when you go to a major hotel or resort, the only black people you see are the ones you brought with you.

It is a fact that black Americans have been part of their own problems, for they have put themselves in a box in many ways. Critics say that black people buy what they do not need and put their hands out for what they do need. To whatever extent this is true, it is part of the image a substantial portion of the population has, and a dilemma of black Americans is that they helped to create the image. Now they must work to undo it. Many key black institutions have crumbled, and many problems remain.

FOR BLACK America and for the larger society, it is time for the next meaningful step in the struggle to address such issues and finally, after more than two centuries, to grant full citizenship to black citizens. It is a time of hope and opportunity, a transitional moment if we make it so. As the political move to the right in the Reagan/Bush years shows, however, it can also be a time of danger. The path from hope to fulfillment remains long and difficult.

A Leadership Forum chaired recently by the Reverend Joseph Lowery developed six principles for evaluating new initiatives for the advancement of the black community. These, we believe, are worthy guides. They are:

1. Fairness, including the protection of civil rights.
2. Family preservation.
3. The enhancement of opportunities for economic advancement.
4. Education to enable blacks to take advantage of current and future job opportunities.
5. A safety net for those severely disadvantaged.
6. Racial justice to guarantee equal application of the law for all Americans.[27]

We have done our best to present in this book an accurate analysis of the current state of black America and to give our conclusions as to what this means and how it should direct our actions. Racism, hate, and discrimination still exist, and given human nature they always will, but these negatives cannot and will not control the future. Victory is within reach if African Americans will rededicate themselves to the cause, stay united, and avoid the temptation to focus on self and neglect the larger responsibilities of community.

The black community in America is in a much stronger position to control its destiny than at any time in its history. It has the political and economic power to revitalize essential institutions, and doing this must be a goal for the immediate future.

This means strengthening the black church; holding and acting on the values of self-sufficiency, responsibility, morality, and unity; improving education; participating effectively in the political system; increasing entrepreneurship and economic advancement; and moving further into a broadened mainstream.

NOTES

Prologue

[1]Applebome, Peter. *Dixie Rising*. New York: Times Books, 1996. p. 214.

Chapter 1.

[1]Applebome, Peter. *Dixie Rising*. New York: Times Books, 1996. p. 69.

[2]Bond, Julian. "Where We've Been, Where We're Going: A Vision of Racial Justice in the 1990's." Vol. 25. *Harvard Civil Rights-Civil Liberties Law Review*. Summer 1990. p. 275.

[3]*Ibid*. p. 375.

[4]Bass, Jack. *Unlikely Heroes*. Tuscaloosa, AL: University of Alabama Press, 1981. pp. 312-314.

[5]*Ibid*. pp. 318-319.

[6]National Urban League, Inc. "The State of Black America 1977." January 11, 1977. (mimeo). p. 8.

[7]*Integrated Education*. "The Carter Administration and Civil Rights: An Assessment of the First 18 Months." Vol. 16 November/ December 1978. p. 9.

[8]Finn, Charles E., Jr. "'Affirmative Action' Under Reagan." *Commentary*. Vol. 73. April 1982. p. 7.

[9]*Ibid*. p. 20.

[10]Bond. *Op. cit*. p. 226.

[11]Ness, Ralph G. "The Civil Rights Legacy of the Reagan Years." *USA Today*. Vol. 118. March 1990. p. 16.

[12]Lycayo, Richard. "I, Too, Sing America." *Time*. October 30, 1995. p. 32.

[13]Lycayo. *Ibid*. p. 91.

[14]Bond. *Op. cit*. p. 282.

[15]Brossard, Mario and Richard Morin. "Leader Popular Among Marchers; But Most Came to Support Black Family, Show Unity, Survey Finds." *The Washington Post*. October 17, 1995. p. A1.

[16]Jordan, Vernon E., Jr. "Passages: 1989-2000 — The Problems of Race." Speech delivered at the ITT Conference, Honolulu, Hawaii, January 30, 1989. In *Vital Speeches of the Day*. Vol. 55. April 15, 1989. p. 407.

[17] *The Cleveland Plain Dealer.* "March Draws Reader Praise, but Few Esteem Farrakhan." October 28, 1995. p. 1E.

[18] Armah, Ester. "Summit Heralds New Era." *The Weekly Journal.* November, 23, 1995. p. 1.

Chapter 2.

[1] Marable, Manning. "The Black Faith of W. E. B. Dubois: Sociocultural and Political Dimensions of Black Religion." *The Southern Quarterly.* Vol 23. Spring 1985. p 12.

[2] Lincoln, C. Eric, and Lawrence H. Mamiya. *The Black Church in the African American Experience.* Durham, NC: Duke University Press, 1990. p. 3.

[3] Marable. *Op. cit.* p. 19.

[4] Lincoln. *Op. cit.* p. 8.

[5] *Ibid.* pp. 7, 17.

[6] Marable. *Op. cit.* p. 19.

[7] Lincoln. *Op. cit.* p. 9.

[8] Lincoln. *Op. cit.* p. 8.

[9] Hayman, John. *Bitter Harvest: Richmond Flowers and the Civil Rights Revolution.* Montgomery: Black Belt Press, 1996. p. 28.

[10] Wexler, Sanford. *The Civil Rights Movement.* New York: Facts on File, 1993. p. 326.

[11] Meier, August, and Elliott Rudwick. *From Plantation to Ghetto.* New York: Hill and Wang, 1966. pp. 3-4.

[12] Meier. *Op. cit.* pp. 227-228.

[13] Lincoln. *Op. cit.* p. 123.

[14] Lincoln. *Op. cit.* p. 124.

[15] Lincoln. *Op. cit.* p. 166.

[16] Lincoln. *Op. cit.* p. 16.

[17] Lincoln. *Op. cit.* p. 348.

[18] "Young Black Men and the Church." *Christian Century.* April 27, 1994. p. 440.

[19] Paris, Peter J. "In the Face of Despair." *Christian Century.* April 27, 1994. p. 438.

[20] "Young Black Men and the Church." *Op. cit.* pp. 439-440.

[21] "Young Black Men and the Church." *Op. cit.* p. 440.

[22] Lincoln. *Op. cit.* pp. 383-384.

[23] Banks, Adelle M. "Middle-Class Black Christians Gravitating Toward Megachurches." *The Birmingham News.* May 17, 1996. p. 3G.

[24] Jones, Lawrence N. "The New Black Church." *Ebony.* November 1992. p. 194.

[25] "Young Black Men." *Op. cit.* p. 439.

[26] Jones. *Op. cit.* p. 192.

[27] "Young Black Men." *Op. cit.* p. 439-440.

[28] Cone, James H. *For My People: Black Theology and the Black Church.* Maryknoll, NY: Orbis Books, 1984. p. 186.

[28]Ostling, Richard N. "Strains on the Heart: U.S. Black Churches Battle Apathy and Threats to their Relevance but also Revel in Renewal." *Time*. November 19, 1990. p. 89.

[30]Cone. *Op. cit.* pp. 8-10.

[31]Cone. *Op. cit.* p. 22.

[32]*Ibid.* p. 203.

[33]Ostling. *Op. cit.* p. 89.

[34]Cone. *Op. cit.* p. 201.

[35]Dumaine, Brian. "Blacks on Blacks." *Fortune*. November 2, 1992. p. 126.

[36]Davenport, Dan. "Parenting" *Better Homes and Gardens*. June 1996. p. 46.

[37]Green, Beverly. "African American Families." *National Forum*. Vol 75. Summer 1995. p. 29.

[38]Lincoln. *Op. cit.* pp. 402-403.

[39]Monroe, Sylvester. "The Gospel of Equity." Time. May 10, 1993. pp. 54-55.

[40]Pellauer, Mary. "Global Vision: An Interview with Andrew Young." *Christian Century*. June 21, 1995. p. 644.

[41]Monroe. *Op. cit.* p. 55.

[42]Dyson, Michael. "Gardner Taylor: Poet Laureat of the Pulpit." *Christian Century*. January 4, 1995. p. 12.

[43]Monroe. *Op. cit.* p. 54.

[44]"Black Churches." *Op. cit.* p. 100.

[45]Nored, Ronald E. *Reweaving the Fabric*. Montgomery, AL: Black Belt Press, 1998.

[46]Nored, Ronald E. "Reweaving the Fabric." *Community-In-Action*. Winter 1998. p. 3.

[47]Cone. *Op. cit.* p. 193.

[48]Pellauer, Mary. *Op. cit.* p. 643.

[49]Institute of Church Administration and Management. "Financing African-American Churches." 1998. p. 1.

[50]Institute. *Op. cit.* p. 100.

Chapter 3.

[1]CPRE Policy Briefs. "Equality in Education : Progress, Problems and Possibilities." New Brunswick, NJ: Consortium for Policy Research in Education, 1991. p. 7.

[2]NCES. *The Condition of Education 1995*. Washington, DC: U. S. Office of Education, National Center for Education Statistics. August 1995. p. 3.

[3]Finn, Chester, Jr. "What to Do About Education: The Schools." *Commentary*. Vol. 98. October 1, 1994. p. 34.

[4]Peterkin, Robert S., and Mary Anne Raywid. "Is the Glass Half Full Yet?" *Journal of Negro Education*. Vol. 63. Winter 1994 p. 1.

[5]NCES. *Op. cit.* August 1995.

[6]Wooldridge, Adrian. "A Comparative View of Education." *The Economist*. November

21-27, 1992. p. 2.

[7]NCES. U. S. Department of Education. *1995 Diget of Education Statistics.* Washington, DC:U. S. Office of Education, National Center for Education Statistics. June 1995. pp. 1-2.

[8]Wooldridge. *Op. cit.* p. 1.

[9]Elders, Joycelyn. "Violence as a Public Health Issue for Children." *Childhood Education.* Vol. 70. Annual Theme Issue 1994. p. 260.

[10]James, Bernard. "School Violence and the Law." *Education Digest.* Vol. 60. May 1995. p. 18.

[11]Elders. *Op. cit.* p. 260.

[12]Harry, Beth, Norma Allen, and Margaret McLaughlin. "Communication Versus Compliance: African American Parents' Involvement in Special Education." *Exceptional Children.* Vol. 61. Fall 1995. p. 364.

[13]*School Facilities: America's Schools Report Differing Conditions.* Washington, DC: United States General Accounting Office, June 14, 1966. pp 1-5.

[14]Odden, Allan. "Including School Finance in Systemic Reform Strategies: A Commentary." New Brunswick, NJ: Consortium for Policy Research in Education, May 1994. p. 3.

[15]Peterkin. *Op. cit.* p. 1.

[16]Schweinhart, Lawrence J. "What the High/Scope Perry Preschool Study Reveals About Development Transitions and Contextual Challenges of Ethnic Males." Paper presented to the annual conference of the American Psychological Asosciation, Toronto, Canada, August 20, 1993. p. 8.

[17]"GOALS 2000." Washington, DC: U.S. Office of Education, 1994. Material obtained from the Office of Education homepage on the World Wide Web.

[18]Odden. *Op. cit.* p. 6.

[19]"Goals 2000." *Op. cit.*

[20]Task Force. "Youth at Work: Making It in the Global Economy." A Report of the At-Risk Youth Task Force. Trenton, NJ: New Jersey Sate Employment and Training Commission, September 1993. p. 6.

[21]Weisburg, Michael, and Eldon J. Ullmer. "Distance Learning Revisited: Life-Long Learning and the National Information Infrastructure." In *Proceedings of the 1995 National Convention of the Association for Educational Communications and Technology.* p. 634.

[22]Paris, Peter J. "In the Face of Despair." *Christian Century.* April 27, 1994. p. 439.

[23]Weisburg. *Op. cit.* p. 6.

[24]CPRE. *Op. cit.* p. 6.

[25]Finn. *Op. cit.* pp. 34-37.

[26]Peterkin. *Op. cit.* p. 3.

[27]Fuhrman, Susan H. "Bringing Systemic Reform to Life." *The Education Digest.* Vol. 60. May 1995. pp. 4-7.

[28]Pitsch, Mark. "Alliance for Learning." *Education Week.* Vol. 13. April 13, 1994. p. 1.

[29]Thornton, Shirley A. "African Americans Moving into the 21st Century: Accepting Responsibility for our Own Destiny." *Journal of Negro Education*. Vol. 64. Spring 1995. p. 105.

[30] CPRE. *Op. cit.* pp. 3-4.

[31]Peterkin. *Op. cit.* p. 1.

[32]Webster, Angela F. "The Consequences of the Lack of Critical Thinking-Based Education in the African American Community." Paper presented at the annual meeting of the Mid-South Educational Research Association, Nashville, TN, November 1994. pp. 6-11.

[33]CPRE. *Op. cit.* p. 7.

[34]Lee, Courtland C. "Empowering Young Black Males." Ann Arbor, MI: ERIC Clearinghouse on Counseling and Personnel Serivces, 1991. p. 2.

[35]Jenifer, Franklyn G. "Between a Rock and a Hard Place." *Journal of Negro Education*. Vol. 61. Winter 1992. p. 2.

[36]Lee. *Op. cit.* p. 3.

[37]Dorman, Arthur, and Others. "Recruiting and Retaining Minority Teachers: A National Perspective." Elmhurst, IL: North Central Regional Educational Laboratory, 1990. p. 4.

[38]Jenifer. *Op. cit.* p. 1.

[39]Leslie, Connie. "You Can't High-Jump if the Bar is Set Low" *Newsweek*. November 6, 1995. p. 82.

[40]Dumaine, Brian. "Blacks on Blacks." *Fortune*. November 2, 1992. p. 123.

[41]Thornton. *Op. cit.* p. 106.

[42]Harris, J. Jerome. "Strategies for Success." *Journal of Negro Education*. Vol. 59. Spring 1990. p. 137.

[43]Hughes, Clarence E. "A Case for the Formation of Strategically Focused Consortia Among HBCU's." *Journal of Negro Education*. Vol. 61. Fall 1992. p. 542.

[44]Task Force. *Op. cit.* p. 13.

[45]Webster. *Op. cit.* pp. 13-16.

[46]Pardini, Priscilla. "Force Parents to be Involved?" *Education Digest*. Vol. 60. May 1995. p. 25.

[47]Schweinhart. *Op. cit.* pp. 2-88.

[48]Foster, Michele. "Savage Inequalities: Where Have We Come From? Where Are We Going?" *Educational Theory*. Vol. 43. Winter 1993. p. 55.

[49]Miller, Julie A. "An Education Revolution." *Education Week*. Special Report. May 22, 1991. pp. C1-C19.

[50]Jenifer. *Op. cit.* pp. 2-3.

Chapter 4.

[1]Bass, Jack. *Unlikely Heroes*. Tuscaloosa, AL: University of Alabama Press, 1981. p. 263.

[2]Laiscell, Ed. "Black Political Empowerment Since Dr. King's Death." *Washington*

Informer. January 17, 1996. p. PG.

[3]Edsall, Thomas, and Mary D. Edsall. "Race." *The Atlantic Monthly.* May 1991. pp. 9-10.

[4]Boyd, Herb. "Henry Louis Gates, Jr., Unveils Four Black Renaissances." *New York Amsterdam News.* November 25, 1995. p. PG.

[5]Carter, Stephen L. "Foreword." *The Tyranny of the Majority.* By Lani Guinier. New York: The Free Press, 1994. p. xiii.

[6]Daniels, Ron. "The African-American Ballot As a Weapon of Struggle." *Black Collegian.* Vol. 21. January 1, 1991. p. 170.

[7]Grier, Peter, and James N. Thurman. "Some Fresh (and Unusual) Faces in '98." *The Christian Science Monitor.* November 5, 1998. p. 18.

[8]Kearney, Eric. "The Supreme Court May Limit African American Representation." *Michigan Chronicle.* January 30, 1996. p. PG.

[9]Marable, Manning. "History and Black Consciousness: The Political Culture of Black America." *Monthly Review.* Vol 47. July 1, 1995. p. 71.

[10]Sunquist, Eric J. "The Talented Tenth." *Commentary.* Vol. 102. July 1, 1996. p. 63.

[11]Marable, Manning. *Op. cit.* p. 71.

[12]Heineman, Robert. "Fin de Siecle Federalism: The Supreme Court and the Redistribution of Constitutional Power." *Perspectives on Political Science.* Vol 22. Summer 1993.

[13]Fulani, Lenora. "Black Empowerment: The Issue is Which White Folks We Work With and What the Objectives and Terms of Coalitions With Them Must Be." *New Pittsburg Courier.* June 29, 1994. p. PG.

[14]Wright, Sharon D. "Electoral and Biracial Coalition: Possible Election Strategy for African American Candidates in Louisville, Kentucky." *Journal of Black Studies.* Vol 25. July 1995. pp. 751-752.

[15]Guinier, Lani. *The Tyranny of the Majority.* New York: The Free Press, 1994. p. 5.

[16]Marable, Manning. *Op. cit.* p. 78.

[17]Coffey, Oscal J. "Leadership And The Problem." *Precinct Reporter.* November 16, 1995. p. 1.

[18]Smith, Errol. "Race and Responsibility." *Reason.* Vol 27. May 1, 1995. p. 61.

[19]Smith, Errol. *Op. cit.* pp. 61, 621.

[20]Smith, Errol. *Op. cit.* p. 62.

[21]Fullwood, Sam III. "For the First Time, A Generation of Black Scholars is Defining What it Means to be an American, and They are Asking Provocative Questions About Class, Gender and Race in the Post-Civil Rights Era." *Los Angeles Times Magazine.* April 9, 1995. p. 12.

[22]Coffey, Oscal J. *Op. cit.* p. 2.

[23]Carter, Stephen L. *Op. cit.* p. xiii.

[24]Bauman, David. "Lockman: No More 'Hand Full of Gimme and a Mouthful of Much Obliged.'" Gannett News Service. p. arc.

[25]Marable, Manning. *Op. cit.* p. 78.

Chapter 5.

[1]Kaplan, Gary. "Put Work Force Training at the Top of the Agenda." *Boston Business Journal*. July 26, 1996. p. 13.

[2]National Institute for Literacy. "What Kind of Adult Literacy Policy Do We Need if We Are Serious About Enabling Every Adult to Become a High Sills/High Wage Worker in the Global Economy?" Washington, DC: National Institute for Literacy, June 1994. Abstract.

[3]Lipset, Seymour, and Ray Marcella. "Technology, Work, and Social Change." *Journal of Labor Research*. Vol. 17. September 1, 1966. p. 613.

[4]Terrey, John N. "Shaping the Curriculum: Values, Community, and a Global Economy." Speech delivered to a meeting of Washington State Community College representatives on April 26, 1991. p. 7.

[5]Halfond, Jay. "Work Force Change Brings Anxiety for Many." *Boston Business Journal*. December 15, 1995. p. 15.

[6]Daggett, Willard R. "Job Skills of 90's Require New Educational Model for All Students." Alexandria, VA: National Association of State Directors of Special Education, 1996. p. 2.

[7]Weinberg, Daniel H. "A Brief Look at Postwar U.S. Income Inequality." Washington, DC: U.S. Department of Commerce, Bureau of the Census. June 1996. pp. 1-3.

[8]Halfond, Jay. "American Almanac Chronicles Our Saga." *Boston Business Journal*. January 1, 1996. p. 15.

[9]Halfond, 1995. *Op. cit.* p. 14.

[10]Bureau of the Census. "How We're Changing: Demographic State of the Nation in 1996." Washington, DC: U.S. Department of Commerce, Bureau of the Census, Special Studies Series P23-191. February 1996. p. 23.

[11]National Institute. *Op. cit.* p. 2.

[12]Lipset. *Op. cit.* p. 614.

[13]Daggett. *Op. cit.* p. 4.

[14]Kerka, Sandra. *Career Education for a Global Economy*. Columbus, OH: ERIC Clearinghouse on Adult, Career, and Volcational education, 1993. p. 3.

[15]Lipset. *Op. cit.* p. 621.

[16]Daggett. *Op. cit.* p. 2.

[17]Ryscavage, Paul. "A Perspective on Low-Wage Workers." Washington, DC: U. S. Department of Commerce, Bureau of the Census, August 1996. p. 5.

[18]Task Force. "Youth at Work: Making It in the Global Economy." A Report of the At-Risk Youth Task Force. Trenton, NJ: New Jersey Sate Employment and Training Commission, September 1993. p. 6.

[19]Daggett. *Op. cit.* pp. 3-4.

[20]Winters, Kirk. "Building Bridges from School to Work. A Background Paper for the Goals 2000: Educate America Satellite Town Meeting." 1993. ERIC Document ED366802. Abstract.

[21]Lerman, Robert I., and Hillard Pouncy. "Why America Should Develop a Youth Apprenticeship System." Washington, DC: Progressive Policy Institute, 1990. Abstract.

[22]Terrey. *Op. cit.* pp. 12-15.

[23]Machaud, Anne. "Only 16 Percent of U.S. Workers Getting Company Training." *Los Angeles Times.* May 18, 1994. p. 1.

[24]Kaplan. *Op. cit.* p. 14.

[25]Lipset. *Op. cit.* p. 613.

[26]Lipset. *Ibid.*

[27]Drucker, Peter F. "The Age of Social Transformation." *Atlantic Monthly.* November 1994. p. 6.

[28]Myers, Samuel L., Jr. "The Evolving Face of Capitalism and Prospects for Black Economic Empowerment." *The Review of Black Political Economy.* Vol. 23. Winter 1995. p. 9.

[29]Drucker. *Op. cit.* p. 6.

[30]Rodriguez, Esther M, and Michael T. Nettles. "Achieving the National Education Goals: The Status of Minorities in Today's Global Economy." Denver, CO: State Higher Education Executive Officers Association, May 1993. p. 13.

[31]Bureau of Labor Statistics, U. S. Department of Labor. *Monthy Labor Review.* November 1977.

[32]Foggo, James G. "Review of Data on Black Americans." Washington, DC: Defense Equal Opportunity Management Institute, 1993. p. 3.

[33]Steele, Claude M. "Race and the Schooling of Black Americans." *The Atlantic Monthly.* April 1992. pp. 67-68.

[34]Rodriguez. *Op. cit.* pp. 14-15.

[35]Eller, Eller, T. J. "Who Stays Poor? Who Doesn't?" Washington, DC: U. S. Department of Commerce, Bureau of the Census, June 1966. pp. 2-5.

[36]Smith, Errol. "Black Separatism — Not Now, Not Ever." *Headway.* January 31, 1996.

[37]Dumaine, Brian. "Blacks on Blacks." *Fortune.* November 2, 1992. p. 122.

Chapter 6.

[1]Ahiarah, Sol. "Black America's Business Ownership Factors: A Theoretical Perspective." *Review of Black Political Economy.* Vol. 22. September 1, 1993. p. 2.

[2]Smith, J. I. *The Buffalo News.* July 8, 1991. p. D-5.

[3]Williams, Roy L. "Columnist: Vital for More Blacks to Own Businesses." *The Birmingham News.* Vol. 109, No. 55. May 17, 1996. p. 3E.

[4]Monroe, Sylvester. "The Gospel of Equity." *Time.* May 10, 1993. p. 55.

[5]Salyers, Eddie. "Black-Owned Business Firms Up 46 Percent Over Five Years, Census Bureau Survey Shows." Washington, DC: U.S. Department of Commerce, Bureau of the Census, 1992. p. 1.

[6]National Black Business Trade Association, Inc. "A Million Men Marched; The

National African American Leadership Summit Met; Now Let's Get Busy!" Press release. June 16, 1996. p. 1.

[7]Davidson, Joe. "Shoplifting Black Dollars. *Emerge, Black America's Newsmagazine*. Vol. 6. March 1995. p. 30.

[8]*Ibid.*

[9]Ahiarah. *Op. cit.* p. 8.

[10]Moeller, Karin. "Top Ten Businesses for 1997." *Business Start-Ups*. Vol. 9. January 1977. p. 22.

[11]Davis, Bob. "A Practical Guide to Creating a Revolving Loan Fund." *Management Quarterly*. Vol. 36. April 1, 1995. p. 7.

[12]Hart, Lylo-Patarick. "Starting Smart." *Business Start-Ups*. Vol. 9. January 1997. p. 64.

[13]Brown, Carolyn M. "Park Your Company Here." *Black Enterprise*. November 30, 1995. p. 3.

[14]Brooks, Nancy Rivera. "Business Incubators Help Reduce the Risk and Costs of Starting a Firm, and They're Rapidly Gaining Popularity." *Los Angeles Times*. November 20, 1996. Business Section. p. 2.

[15]Brown. *Op. cit.* p. 2.

[16]Day, Bill. "How to Nurture an Idea Into An Enterprise. *De Moines Business Record*. June 3, 1996. p. 1.

[17]Brown. *Op. cit.* p. 3.

[18]Brown. *Op. cit.* pp. 1-4.

[19]Ahiarah. *Op. cit.* p. 11.

[20]Davidson. *Ibid.*

[21]Davidson. *Op. cit.* pp. 28-29.

[22]Ahiarah. *Op. cit.* p. 4-5.

[23]Davidson. *Op. cit.* pp. 28-30.

[24]Davidson. *Ibid.*

[25]Davidson. *Op. cit.* pp. 28-30.

[26]National. *Op. cit.* p. 1.

[27]Clements, Dawn A. "Entrepreneur As Advocate." *Minority Business Entrepreneur*. December 31, 1995. pp. 3-5.

[28]Sterling, H. Dwight. "Harvard Divinity Student Says The Black Church is Key to Revitalizing." *Oakland Post*. September 19, 1993. pp. 1-2.

Chapter 7.

[1]Jordan, Vernon E., Jr. "Passages: 1989-2000 — The Problems of Race." Speech delivered at the ITT Conference, Honolulu, Hawaii, January 30, 1989. In *Vital Speeches of the Day*. Vol. 55. April 15, 1989. p. 408.

[2]Marable, Manning. *Along the Color Line*. Audio Series. November 1996.

[3]Hughes, Clarence E. "A Case for the Foundation of Strategically Focused Consortia Among HBCUs." *Journal of Negro Education*. Vol. 61. Fall 1992. p. 541.

[5]*Ibid.*

[5]Abu-Jamal, Mumia. "Retiree Continues Mission of Teaching African Heritage." *Michigan Citizen.* December 31, 1994. p. 1.

[6]Abu-Jamal, Mumia. "Of Marches and Men." *Michigan Citizen.* December 9, 1995. p. 3.

[7]Hayman, John L, Jr. "Attitudes and Attitude Measurement in Education." San Francisco: Far West Laboratory for Educational Research and Development, 1975. p. 25.

[8]Herbert, Bob. "Saving the Cities." *New York Times.* July 2, 1998. editorial section.

[9]"New Low for Out-of-Wedlock Black Births." *New York Times.* July 1, 1998. p. 1.

[10]Westphal, David. *The Birmingham News.* October 10, 1998. p. C12.

[11]Edsall, Thomas Byrne, and Mary D. Edsall. "Race." *The Atlantic Monthly.* May 1991. p. 9.

[12]Hughes. *Op. cit.* pp. 541-542.

[13]Fullwood, Sam III. "For the First Time, A Generation of Black Scholars is Defining What it Means to be an American, and They are Asking Provocative Questions About Class, Gender and Race in the post-Civil Rights Era." *Los Angeles Times Magazine.* April 9, 1995. p. 14.

[14]Fulani, Lenora. "Black Empowerment: The Issue is Which White Folks We Work With and What the Objectives and Terms of Coalitions With them Must Be." *New Pittsburg Courier.* June 29, 1994. pp. PG.

[15]Lomax, Louis. *Revolt,* p. 264.

[16]Lincoln. p. 125.

[17]Lincoln. *Op. cit.* p. 7.

[18]Smith, Errol. "Black Separatism — Not Now, Not Ever." *Headway.* January 31, 1996. p. PG.

[19]Ahiarah, Sol. "Black America's Business Ownership Factors: A Theoretical Perspective." *Review of Black Political Economy.* Vol. 22. September 1, 1993. pp. 5-6.

[20]Thornton, Shirley A. "African Americans Moving into the 21st Century: Accepting Responsibility for our Own Destiny." *Journal of Negro Education.* Vol. 64. Spring 1995. pp. 105-106.

[21]Drucker, Peter F. "The Age of Social Transformation." *Atlantic Monthly.* November 1994. p. 5.

[22]Topolnicki, Denise M. "No More Pity for the Poor. Yes, the Welfare System is Broken. But the G.O.P.'s 'Tough Love' Reform Will Not Reduce the Poverty Rate Unless it Confronts the Myths About the Poor." *Money.* May 1, 1995. p. 124.

[23]Topolnicki. *Op. cit.* p. 122.

[24]Topolnicki. *Op. cit.* p. 124.

[25]Nader, Ralph. "It's Time to End Corporate Welfare As We Know It." Speech delivered at Haverford College in 1995. pp. 1-2.

[26]Jacob, John E. "Black America, 1989: An Overview." *The State of Black America 1990.* New York: National Urban League, Inc., 1990. p. 7.

[27]Myers, Samuel L., Jr. "The Evolving Face of Capitalism and Prospects for Black

Economic Empowerment." *The Review of Black Political Economy*. Vol. 23. Winter 1995. p. 11.

BIBLIOGRAPHY

Abu-Jamal, Mumia. "Of Marches and Men." Michigan *Citizen*. December 9, 1995. 3 pp.

Abu-Jamal, Mumia. "Retiree Continues Mission of Teaching African Heritage." *Michigan Citizen*. December 31, 1994. 3 pp.

Ahiarah, Sol. "Black America's Business Ownership Factors: A Theoretical Perspective." *Review of Black Political Economy*. Vol. 22. September 1, 1993. 15 pp.

Applebome, Peter. *Dixie Rising*. New York: Times Books, 1996. 385 pp.

Armah, Ester. "Summit Heralds New Era." *The Weekly Journal*. November, 23, 1995. p. 1.

Arrington, Richard. "Black Community Crusade for Children; The Value of Self-Expectations." *The Birmingham Times*. Vol. 31. May 2, 1996. p. 2.

Banks, Adelle M. "Middle-Class Black Christians Gravitating Toward Megachurches." *The Birmingham News*. Vol. 109. May 17, 1996. pp. 1G-3G.

Bass, Jack. *Unlikely Heroes*. Tuscaloosa, AL: University of Alabama Press, 1981. 352 pp.

Bauman, David. "Lockman: No More 'Hand Full of Gimme and a Mouthful of Much Obliged.'" Gannett News Service. June 6, 1996.

"Black Churches in Business." *The Christian Century*. January 31, 1996. p. 100.

Bond, Julian. "Where We've Been, Where We're Going: A Vision of Racial Justice in the 1990's." *Harvard Civil Rights-Civil Liberities Law Review*. Vol. 25. Summer 1990. pp. 273-285.

Boyd, Herb. "Henry Louis Gates, Jr., Unveils Four Black Renaissances." *New York Amsterdam News*. November 25, 1995. pp PG.

Brooks, Nancy Rivera. "Business Incubators Help Reduce the Risk and

Costs of Starting a Firm, and They're Rapidly Gaining Popularity." *Los Angeles Times.* November 20, 1996. Business Section, p. 2.

Brossard, Mario and Richard Morin. "Leader Popular Among Marchers; But Most Came to Support Black Family, Show Unity, Survey Finds." *The Washington Post.* October 17, 1995. p. A1.

Brown, Carolyn M. "Park Your Company Here." *Black Enterprise.* November 30,1995. 5 pp.

Bureau of the Census. "How We're Changing: Demographic State of the Nation in 1996." Washington, DC: U.S. Department of Commerce, Bureau of the Census, Special Studies Series P23-191. February 1996. 4 pp.

Bureau of Labor Statistics, U. S. Department of Labor. Monthy Labor Review. November 1977.

Carter, Stephen L. "Forward." *The Tyranny of the Majority.* By Lani Guinier. New York: The Free Press, 1994. pp. vii-xx.

Cheatham, Janet, ed. *Famous Black Quotations.* New York, NY: Warner Books, 1986. p. 12.

Clements, Dawn A. "Entrepreneur As Advocate." *Minority Business Entrepreneur.* December 31, 1995. 5 pp.

Coffey, Oscal J. "Leadership And The Problem." *Precinct Reporter.* November 16, 1995. pp. 1-3.

Cone, James H. *For My People: Black Theology and the Black Church.* Maryknoll, NY: Orbis Books, 1984. 271pp.

CPRE Policy Briefs. "Equality in Education: Progress, Problems and Possibilities." New Brunswick, NJ: Consortium for Policy Research in Education, 1991. xx pp.

Daggett, Willard R. "Job Skills of 90's Require New Educational Model for All Students." Alexandria, VA: National Association of State Directors of Special Education, 1996. 19 pp.

Daniels, Ron. "The African-American Ballot As a Weapon of Struggle." *Black Collegian.* Vol. 21. January 1, 1991. pp. 168-171.

Davenport, Dan. "Parenting." *Better Homes and Gardens.* Vol. 74. June

1996. pp. 46-51.

Davidson, Joe. "Shoplifting Black Dollars. *Emerge, Black America's Newsmagazine.* Vol. 6. March 1995. pp. 28-30.

Davis, Bob. "A Practical Guide to Creating a Revolving Loan Fund." *Management Quarterly.* Vol. 36. April 1, 1995. 24 pp.

Day, Bill. "How to Nurture an Idea Into An Enterprise." *Des Moines Business Record.* June 3, 1996. 12 pp.

Dorman, Arthur, and Others. "Recruiting and Retaining Minority Teachers: A National Perspective." Elmhurst, Il: North Central Regional Educational Laboaratory, 1990. 10 pp.

Drucker, Peter F. "The Age of Social Transformation." *Atlantic Monthly.* November 1994. pp. 53-72.

Dyson, Michael. "Gardner Taylor: Poet Laureat of the Pulpit." *Christian Century.* January 4, 1995. pp. 12-20.

Dumaine, Brian. "Blacks on Blacks." *Fortune.* November 2, 1992. pp. 118-132.

Edsall, Thomas Byrne, and Mary D. Edsall. "Race." *The Atlantic Monthly.* May 1991. pp. 53-86.

Elders, Joycelyn. "Violence as a Public Health Issue for Children." *Childhood Education.* Vol. 70. Annual Theme Issue 1994. pp. 260-262.

Eller, T. J. "Who Stays Poor? Who Doesn't?" Washington, DC: U. S. Department of Commerce, Bureau of the Census, June 1966. 6 pp.

Feldman, Linda. *The Christian Science Monitor.* November 5, 1998. p. 18.

Finn, Charles E., Jr. "'Affirmative Action' Under Reagan." *Commentary.* Vol. 73. April 1982. pp. 17-28.

Finn, Chester E., Jr.. "Towards Excellence in Education." *Public Interest.* Vol. 120. June 1, 1995. pp. 41-19.

Finn, Chester, Jr. "What to Do About Education: The Schools." *Commentary.* Vol. 98. October 1, 1994. pp 30-39.

Foggo, James G. "Review of Data on Black Americans." Washington,

DC: Defense Equal Opportunity Management Institute, 1993. 20 pp.

Foster, Michele. "Savage Inequalities: Where Have We Come From? Where Are We Going?" *Educational Theory*. Vol. 43. Winter 1993. pp 23-32.

Fuhrman, Susan H. "Bringing Systemic Reform to Life." *The Education Digest*. Vol. 60. May 1995. pp. 4-8.

Fulani, Lenora. "Black Empowerment: The Issue is Which White Folks We Work With and What the Objectives and Terms of Coalitions With them Must Be." *New Pittsburg Courier*. June 29, 1994. pp. PG.

Fullwood, Sam III. "For the First Time, A Generation of Black Scholars is Defining What it Means to be an American, and They are Asking Provocative Questions About Class, Gender and Race in the Post-Civil Rights Era." *Los Angeles Times Magazine*. April 9, 1995. pp. 10-18.

"GOALS 2000." Washington, DC: U.S. Office of Education, 1994. Material obtained from the Office of Education homepage on the World Wide Web.

Grant, Linda, and Robert F. Black. "Getting Business Off the Dole." *U.S. News & World Report*. April 10, 1995. p. 38.

Green, Beverly. "African American Families." *National Forum*. Vol 75. Summer 1995. pp. 29-32.

Grier, Peter, and James N. Thurman. "Some Fresh (and Unusual) Faces in '98." *The Christian Science Monitor*. November 5, 1998. pp. 1,18.

Guinier, Lani. *The Tyranny of the Majority*. New York: The Free Press, 1994. 324 pp.

Halfond, Jay. "Work Force Change Brings Anxiety for Many." *Boston Business Journal*. Vol. 15. December 15, 1995. pp 14-15.

Halfond, Jay. "American Almanac Chronicles Our Saga." *Boston Business Journal*. Vol 15. January 1, 1996. pp 14-15.

Harris, J. Jerome. "Strategies for Success." *Journal of Negro Education*. Vol. 59. Spring 1990. pp. 134-138.

Harry, Beth, Norma Allen, and Margaret McLaughlin. "Communication Versus Compliance: African American Parents' Involvement in Special Education." *Exceptional Children*. Vol. 61. Fall 1995. pp. 364-377.

Hart, Lylo-Patarick. "Starting Smart." *Business Start-Ups*. Vol. 9. January 1997. p. 64.

Hayman, John L, Jr. "Attitudes and Attitude Measurement in Education." San Francisco: Far West Laboratory for Educational Research and Development, 1975. 64 pp. monograph.

Hayman, John. *Bitter Harvest: Richmond Flowers and the Civil Rights Revolution*. Montgomery: Black Belt Press, 1996. 350 pp.

Heineman, Robert. "Fin de Siecle Federalism: The Supreme Court and the Redistribution of Constitutional Power." *Perspectives on Political Science*. Vol 22. Summer 1993. pp. 102-109.

Hughes, Clarence E. "A Case for the Formation of Strategically Focused Consortia Among HBCU's." *Journal of Negro Education*. Vol. 61. Fall 1992. pp. 539-553.

"Income Disparity Between Poorest and Richest Rises." *New York Times*. June 20, 1996.

Institute of Church Administration and Management. "Financing African-American Churches." Report of a National Survey on Church Giving. Atlanta: Interdenominational Theological Center, 1998. 180.

Integrated Education. "The Carter Administration and Civil Rights: An Assessment of the First 18 Months." Vol. 16. November/ December 1978. pp. 9-19.

Jacob, John E. "Black America, 1989: An Overview." *The State of Black America 1990*. New York: National Urban League, Inc., 1990. pp. 1-8.

James, Bernard. "School Violence and the Law." *Education Digest*. Vol. 60. May 1995. pp. 17-20.

Jennifer, Franklyn G. "Between a Rock and a Hard Place." Journal of

Negro Education. Vol. 61. Winter 1992. pp. 1-3.

Johnson, Olin Chester. *The Black Church in America.* 1975. ERIC document ED107576. 8 pp.

Jones, Lawrence N. "The New Black Church." *Ebony.* Vol. 48. November 1992. pp 192-194.

Jordan, Vernon E., Jr. "Passages: 1989-2000 — The Problems of Race." Speech delivered at the ITT Conference, Honolulu, Hawaii, January 30, 1989. In *Vital Speeches of the Day.* Vol. 55. April 15, 1989. pp. 406-408.

Kaplan, Gary. "Put Work Force Training at the Top of the Agenda." *Boston Business Journal.* Vol. 16. July 26, 1996. pp 13-15.

Kearney, Eric. "The Supreme Court May Limit African American Representation." *Michigan Chronicle.* January 30, 1996. pp. PG.

Kerka, Sandra. *Career Education for a Global Economy.* Columbus, OH: ERIC Clearinghouse on Adult, Career, and Vocational education, 1993. 4 pp.

Kirp, David L. "Faded Dreams: The Politics and Economics of Race in America." *The Nation.* April 24, 1995. pp. 567-572.

Laiscell, Ed. "Black Political Empowerment Since Dr. King's Death." *Washington Informer.* January 17, 1996. pp. PG.

Lee, Courtland C. "Empowering Young Black Males." Ann Arbor, MI: ERIC Clearinghouse on Counseling and Personnel Serivces, 1991. 3 pp.

Lerman, Robert I., and Hillard Pouncy. "Why America Should Develop a Youth Apprenticeship System." Washington, DC: Progressive Policy Institute, 1990.

Leslie, Connie. "You Can't High-Jump if the Bar is Set Low." *Newsweek.* November 6, 1995. p. 82.

Lincoln, C. Eric, and Lawrence H. Mamiya. *The Black Church in the African American Experience.* Durham, NC: Duke University Press, 1990. 519 pp.

Lipset, Seymour, and Ray Marcella. "Technology, Work, and Social

Change." *Journal of Labor Research*. Vol. 17. September 1, 1966. pp. 613-629.

Lomax, Louis E. *The Negro Revolt*. New York: Signet Books, 1962. 288 pp.

Lycayo, Richard. "I, Too, Sing America." *Time*. October 30, 1995. p. 32.

Machaud, Anne. "Only 16 Percent of U.S. Workers Getting Company Training." *Los Angeles Times*. May 18, 1994. pp. D-1.

Marable, Manning. "History and Black Consciousness: The Political Culture of Black America." *Monthly Review*. Vol 47. July 1, 1995. pp.71-80.

Marable, Manning. "The Black Faith of W. E. B. Dubois: Sociocultural and Political Dimensions of Black Religion." *The Southern Quarterly*. Vol 23. Spring 1985. pp 15-33.

Marable, Manning. *Along the Color Line*. Audio Series. November 1996.

Meier, August, and Elliott Rudwick. *From Plantation to Ghetto*. New York: Hill and Wang, 1966. 340 pp.

Miller, Julie A. "An Education Revolution." *Education Week*. Special Report. May 22, 1991. pp. C1-C19.

Moeller, Karin. "Top Ten Businesses for 1997." *Business Start-Ups*. Vol. 9. January 1977. pp. 22-31

Monroe, Sylvester. "The Gospel of Equity." *Time*. Vol. 141. May 10, 1993. pp. 54-55.

Myers, Samuel L., Jr. "The Evolving Face of Capitalism and Prospects for Black Economic Empowerment." *The Review of Black Political Economy*. Vol. 23. Winter 1995. pp. 5-12.

Nader, Ralph. "It's Time to End Corporate Welfare As We Know It." Speech delivered at Haverford College in 1995.

National Black Business Trade Association, Inc. "A Million Men Marched; The National African American Leadership Summit Met; Now Let's Get Busy!" Press release, June 16, 1996.

National Institute for Literacy. "What Kind of Adult Literacy Policy Do

We Need if We Are Serious About Enabling Every Adult to Become a High Sills/High Wage Worker in the Global Economy?" Washington, DC: National Institute for Literacy, June 1994. 10 pp.

NCES. The Condition of Education 1995. Washington, DC: U. S. Office of Education, National Center for Education Statistics. August 1995.

NCES. U. S. Department of Education. 1995 Diget of Education Statistics. Washington, DC:U. S. Office of Education, National Center for Education Statistics. June 1995.

Ness, Ralph G. "The Civil Rights Legacy of the Reagan Years." *USA Today*. Vol. 118. March 1990. pp. 16-18.

Nored, Ronald E. *Reweaving the Fabric*. Montgomery, AL: Black Belt Press, 1998.

Nored, Ronald E. "Reweaving the Fabric." *Community-In-Action*. Winter 1998. p. 3.

Odden, Allan. "Including School Finance in Systemic Reform Strategies: A Commentary." New Brunswick, NJ: Consortium for Policy Research in Education, May 1994. 13 pp.

Ostling, Richard N. "Strains on the Heart: U.S. Black Churches Battle Apathy and Threats to their Relevance but also Revel in Renewal." *Time*. November 19, 1990. pp. 88-89.

Pardini, Priscilla. "Force Parents to be Involved?" *Education Digest*. Vol. 60. May 1995. pp 20-25.

Paris, Peter J. "In the Face of Despair." *Christian Century*. Vol. 111. April 27, 1994. pp. 438-439.

Pellauer, Mary. "Global Vision: An Interview with Andrew Young." *Christian Century*. June 21, 1995. pp. 638-644.

Peterkin, Robert S., and Mary Anne Raywid. "Is the Glass Half Full Yet?" *Journal of Negro Education*. Vol. 63. Winter 1994 pp. 1-4.

Pitsch, Mark. "Alliance for Learning." *Education Week*. Vol. 13. April 13, 1994. 20 pp.

Riley, Dorothy Winbush, ed. *My Soul Looks Back, 'Less I Forget: A*

Collection of Quotations by People of Color. New York: Harper Collins, 1993. p. 58.

Rodriguez, Esther M, and Michael T. Nettles. "Achieving the National Education Goals: The Status of Minorities in Today's Global Economy." Denver, CO: State Higher Education Executive Officers Association, May 1993. 24 pp.

Ryscavage, Paul. "A Perspective on Low-Wage Workers." Washington, DC: U. S. Department of Commerce, Bureau of the Census, August 1996. 7 pp.

Salyers, Eddie. "Black-owned Business Firms Up 46 Percent Over Five Years, Census Bureau Survey Shows." Washington, DC: U.S. Department of Commerce, Bureau of the Census, 1992. 2 pp.

School Facilities: America's Schools Report Differing Conditions. Washington, DC: United States General Accounting Office, June 14, 1966. 105 pp.

Schweinhart, Lawrence J. "What the High/Scope Perry Preschool Study Reveals About Development Transitions and Contextual Challenges of Ethnic Males." Paper presented to the annual conference of the American Psychological Asosciation, Toronto, Canada, August 20, 1993. 12 pp.

Smith, Errol. "Black Separatism — Not Now, Not Ever." *Headway.* January 31, 1996.

Smith, Errol. "Race and Responsibility." *Reason.* Vol 27. May 1, 1995. pp. 60-65.

Smith, J. I. *The Buffalo News.* July 8, 1991. p. D-5.

Steele, Claude M. "Race and the Schooling of Black Americans." *The Atlantic Monthly.* April 1992. pp. 67-78.

Sterling, H. Dwight. "Harvard Divinity Student Says The Black Church is Key to Revitalizing." *Oakland Post.* September 19, 1993. 3 pp.

Sunquist, Eric J. "The Talented Tenth." *Commentary.* Vol 102. July 1, 1996. pp. 60-64.

Task Force. "Youth at Work: Making It in the Global Economy." A

Report of the At-Risk Youth Task Force. Trenton, NJ: New Jersey Sate Employment and Training Commission, September 1993. 24 pp.

Terrey, John N. "Shaping the Curriculum: Values, Community, and a Global Economy." Speech delivered to a meeting of Washington State Community College representatives on April 26, 1991. 14 pp.

The Cleveland Plain Dealer. "March Draws Reader Praise, but Few Esteem Farrakhan." October 28, 1995. p. 1E.

Thornton, Shirly A. "Africa Americans Moving into the 21st Century: Accepting Responsibility for our Own Destiny." Journal of Negro Education. Vol. 64. Spring 1995. pp. 104-111.

Topolnicki, Denise M. "No More Pity for the Poor. Yes, the Welfare System is Broken. But the G.O.P.'s 'Tough Love' Reform Will Not Reduce the Poverty Rate Unless it Confronts the Myths About the Poor." Money. May 1, 1995. pp. 122-125.

"Young Black Men and the Church" Christian Century. April 27, 1994. pp. 439-440.

Webster, Angela F. "The Consequences of the lack of Critical Thinking-Based Education in the African American Community." Paper presented at the annual meeting of the Mid-South Educational Research Association, Nashville, TN, November 1994. 25 pp.

Weinberg, Daniel H. "A Brief Look at Postwar U.S. Income Inequality." Washington, DC: U.S. Department of Commerce, Bureau of the Census, 4 pp. June 1996.

Weisburg, Michael, and Eldon J. Ullmer. "Distance Learning Revisited: Life-Long Learning and the National Information Infrastructure." In Proceedings of the 1995 National Convention of the Association for Educational Communications and Technology. pp. 628-647.

Westphal, David. "Black Incomes Soar." The Birmingham News. October 10, 1998. p. C12.

Wexler, Sanford. The Civil Rights Movement. New York: Facts on File, 1993. 356 pp.

Williams, Roy L. "Columnist: Vital for More Blacks to Own Businesses." *The Birmingham News.* Vol. 109. May 17, 1996. pp. 1E-3E.

Winters, Kirk. "Building Bridges from School to Work. A Background
Paper for the Goals 2000: Educate America Satellite Town Meeting."
1993. ERIC Document ED366802.

Wright, Sharon D. "Electoral and Biracial Coalition: Possible Election
Strategy for African American Candidates in Lousiville, Kentucky."
Journal of Black Studies. Vol 25. July 1995. pp. 749-758.

About the Authors

JESSE J. LEWIS, born on a tenant farm, earned four degrees, became a college president, and was the first African American since Reconstruction to serve in the cabinet of an Alabama governor. He is founder of the oldest black-owned advertising and public relations firm in America and owns and publishes the largest black-owned weekly newspaper in the Southeast. Lewis is nationally known in media circles and is Vice-President of the National Black Publishers Association. He is active in political affairs and is a close advisor to Birmingham Mayor Richard Arrington.

JOHN HAYMAN taught at the university level for 20 years and was director of research for Denver and Philadelphia public school systems. From 1991 to 1994, he was Informatics Research director for the International Association of Universities in Paris. He has published more than 60 articles and five books, including *Bitter Harvest: Richmond Flowers and the Civil Rights Revolution* [Black Belt Press, 1996], which won the C. J. Coley prize for history and was a runner-up for the 1997 Robert F. Kennedy Award.